The English Texans

Thomas W. Cutrer

The University of Texas
Institute
of Texan Cultures
at San Antonio

1985

The English Texans
by Thomas W. Cutrer
Copyright ©1985
The University of Texas Institute of Texan Cultures at San Antonio

Jack R. Maguire, Executive Director

Production Staff: Sandra Hodsdon Carr; David Haynes; Meredith Rees; Tom Shelton; Deborah Large, indexer

Library of Congress Catalog Card Number 85-50542

International Standard Book Numbers
Hardbound 0-86701-012-6
Softbound 0-86701-013-4

First Edition

This publication was made possible in part by the Houston Endowment, Inc.

Printed in the United States of America

The English Texans

THE TEXIANS AND THE TEXANS

A series dealing with the many peoples who have contributed to the history and heritage of Texas. Now in print:

Pamphlets—*The Afro-American Texans, The Anglo-American Texans, The Belgian Texans, The Chinese Texans, The Czech Texans, The French Texans, The Greek Texans, The Indian Texans, The Italian Texans, The Jewish Texans, The Mexican Texans, Los Tejanos Mexicanos* (in Spanish), *The Norwegian Texans, The Spanish Texans* and *The Swiss Texans.*

Books—*The Danish Texans, The English Texans, The German Texans, The Irish Texans, The Polish Texans* and *The Wendish Texans.*

Contents

Preface:
Ingram's Walk

On the second day of October in the year 1567, Captain Sir John Hawkins set sail from the English port of Plymouth on his third slaving expedition to Africa and the New World. After making his first landfall on the coast of Guinea, where he traded for a cargo of blacks, Hawkins steered for the Spanish colonies of South America and there exchanged his store of slaves for Peruvian gold. Having turned a handsome profit, the English captain turned his little fleet for home. As the six ships were clearing the Caribbean, however, they were struck by a powerful storm and driven into the Gulf of Mexico.

The English took shelter in the harbor of Veracruz, where they paused to refit and resupply, when they were attacked by a squadron of the Spanish navy. Four of Hawkins's ships were immediately sunk. Of the two remaining, the *Judith*, commanded by the youthful Francis Drake, sailed straight for England, arriving there with no further mishap. The *Minion*, however, under the direct command of Captain Hawkins, was overburdened with English sailors picked from Veracruz harbor after their disastrous fight with the Spanish and was pitifully under-supplied for a voyage across the Atlantic.[1] "With manie sorrowful hearts wee wandred in an unknowen Sea by the space of fourteene dayes," Hawkins reported, "tyll hunger enforced us to seeke the lande. . . ."[2]

The defeat of Sir John Hawkins at San Juan de Ulloa, 1568

At their own request 114 English mariners were set ashore some 30 miles to the north of Tampico in the Spanish province of New Spain. They resolved to face the uncertain dangers of a wild and unexplored continent rather than hazard themselves at sea where they believed that "if they perished not by drowning, yet hunger would inforce them in the ende to eate one another."[3] So began one of the most incredible adventures yet to befall civilized man: an 11-month trek across 3,000 miles of often hostile wilderness. Only three of the 114 survived to return to England. Of these three, only one, David Ingram, was alive to report to English authorities in 1582.

David Ingram's narrative of his singular experience, a walk from Tampico to Cape Breton, off Nova Scotia, inflamed the imagination of the English-speaking world and opened its eyes to the great riches and scenic wonders of the land to the north of the River of May—the land we now know as Texas. Ingram was astounded by its vast size, its unexploited wealth and its great natural beauty, and, like many others who have come under its spell, he was wont to exaggerate its already fabulous resources. In his journey across Texas Ingram reportedly saw "great rockes of Chrystal, Rubies, being four inches long, and two inches broad," a "great aboundance of pearls," "sundry pieces of golde some as big as a man's fist" and other precious minerals by the shipload.[4] Ingram was not only the first Englishman to visit Texas, but the first Texas braggart in the English tongue.

Much of what Ingram reported to Queen Elizabeth's ministers, however, was strictly accurate and no less fabulous. There were, in this land to the north of the River of May — known to the Spaniards as the Rio Bravo del Norte and to later English-speaking visitors as the Rio Grande — "great pleanty of Buffes, Beares, Horses, Kine, Woolves, Foxes, Deare, Goats, Sheeps, Hares, and Conies." The hides of the beasts, said Ingram, "are good Marchandize,"[5] a recommendation which went unheeded by his countrymen until the middle of the 19th century.

More important, the "ground of the Country is most excellent, fertile and pleasant," except to the south where the grass is "burnt away

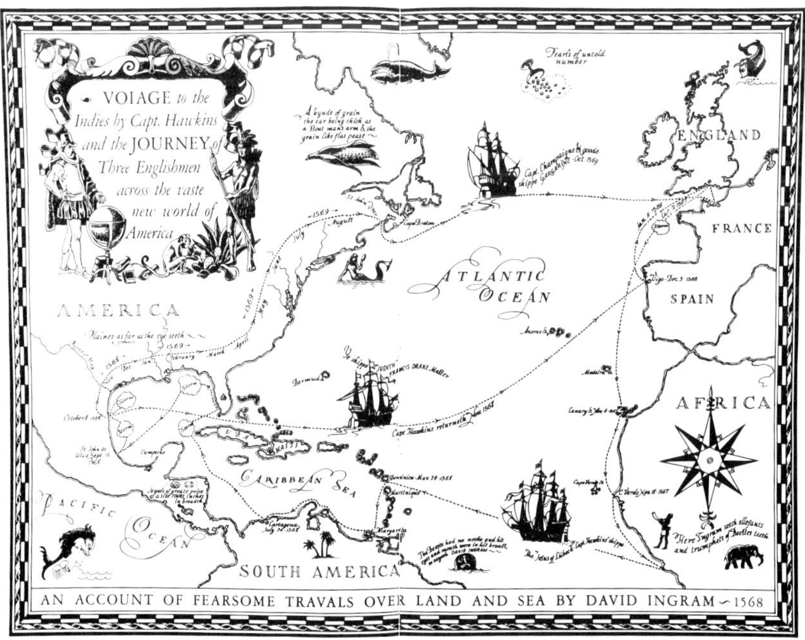

Hawkins' voyage to the Indies and Ingram's Walk, 1568

with the heate of the Sunne." Ingram was most impressed by the great diversity of the land and by its richness. All of the country, he told Queen Elizabeth's ministers, "is good and most delicate, having great plaines, as large and as fayre in many places as may be seen." There were also "great huge woods" in this place "of sundry kinds of trees" and along the vast rivers was luxurious grass which "groweth faster then it can be eaten."[6]

The "Relation of David Ingram of Barking, in the Countie of Essex, Sayler," for all of its wondrous account of the land between the Rio Grande and the Sabine rivers, was little noted when the English began their exploration and settlement in the New World. They were relatively late in their colonizing efforts in the western hemisphere. By 1607, when the first permanent English colony was founded at Jamestown, Virginia, France had a solid claim to the lands watered by the St. Lawrence to the north. Spain, the preeminent colonizer of the 15th and 16th centuries, had a firm grasp on South America and Mexico, and a legal claim, if not a thriving settlement, on all of Texas. Indeed, the Gulf of Mexico was a Spanish lake on which all other nations sailed at their own risk.

Spanish domination of the Gulf ended, however, with the end of the Seven Years' War. The Treaty of Paris of 1763 brought the English occupation of East and West Florida, thus creating a permanent threat to Spanish possessions ringing the Gulf of Mexico. Sensing its military weakness, the Spanish government ordered reinforcements to its coastal garrisons and fortification of points vulnerable to English attack. Of all Spain's New World colonies, Texas was most lightly defended and closest to British naval bases, and so was viewed as the most likely target for English expansionism. With its few Spanish subjects constantly beset by Indian raiders from the north, Texas had only limited resources for repelling an anticipated English invasion.

In the late 1760's English ships intruded into Texas waters with increasing regularity. Although these were only merchant vessels seeking trade in furs with local Indians, Spanish officials became increasingly sensitive to pressure from their English rivals. In April of 1769 the English schooner *Britain* was seized by the Spanish garrison of the Presidio la Bahía in Matagorda Bay.[7]

In 1772 Englishmen were reported among the Indians near Natchitoches, Louisiana, and along the Trinity River, people and lands claimed by the King of Spain. From Mexico City the viceroy ordered an investigation of these English incursions, and soldiers sent out from La Bahía discovered English arms in the possession of the Indians, but could find no Englishmen.[8]

Two years later the viceroy received word that a shipload of Englishmen had remained on the Neches River long enough to raise a crop, and in 1777 a second English vessel, this one loaded with bricks, ran aground and was abandoned in that same river. Another Spanish expedition to locate and expel the interloping English found only a single English sailor who claimed to have been marooned from a passing Jamaican vessel.[9]

These incidents may indicate only a casual exploration of the coast by the British navy or an attempt, as the bricks would suggest, to found a colony or trading post in Texas as early as the time of the American Revolution. In any case, rumors of the presence of English ships and seamen on their northeast frontier stirred considerable interest among the Spanish officials in Mexico and contributed, no doubt, to the already bitter enmity between these two great colonial rivals.

Another 50 years would pass, however, before the Spanish fear of English-speaking aliens implanting colonies in the land beyond the Rio Bravo would become reality. By that time Mexico had become an independent republic, and the "Englishmen" who crossed the Sabine into the Mexican province of Texas were English in ancestry, language and tradition only. Although a late starter in the race for sovereignty of the New World's northern continent, England dominated the trade and capital, language and literature, religion and bureaucracy of the Atlantic coast of North America. Despite the successful revolution of her colonies in 1776 and the inevitable modifications caused by distance and dispersion, the culture of the United States remained unmistakably English well into the national period.

Even after the revolution, English immigrants were welcome in their former colonies. There they found institutions similar, if not identical, to the ones that they had left behind. Not only did the United States and England share a common language, but Englishmen found representative government, Protestant churches and a system of common law in the new republic to be familiar. The Americans' most revered military institution—the militia—and best-established military tradition—the fear of a standing army—both came from England and were to have a forceful impact upon Texas's development and revolt from Mexico. As historian Charlotte Erickson has pointed out, "English immigrants regarded themselves as belonging to the same ethnic stock as a majority of the native-born whites, and they met few obstacles to participation in the same social and institutional life."[10] The English immigrant to the United States was, in fact, so quickly assimilated into the existing culture that a sense of identity with the old country and of ethnic difference from the people of the new rarely existed past the second generation. Thus, by the year 1821, when Stephen F. Austin began to lead American colonists into Texas, the English among them were often invisible as immigrants, and their children were largely indistinguishable from those of the native-born white population.

The Last of England *by Ford Madox Brown*

Chapter 1
Revolution and Republic

The winter of 1820-1821 found Connecticut-born impresario Moses Austin in San Antonio seeking permission of the Spanish authorities to settle 300 American families in the Mexican province of Texas. Permission was granted, but Moses Austin died the following summer, leaving the ambitious undertaking to his son Stephen. Although Mexico's successful revolt against Spanish rule and the unsettled conditions which followed Mexican independence delayed confirmation of the Austin land grant and threw many obstacles into the path of the colonization effort, many other factors favored the Anglo-American settlement of Texas. A long depression, followed by the panic of 1819, had left many Americans financially ruined and eager to make a fresh start on the western frontier. A new and more costly United States policy of private acquisition of public lands discouraged many Americans from seeking titles to homesteads within the bounds of the Louisiana Purchase, and tales of the riches of the land beyond the Sabine were already reaching fabulous proportions in the eastern states. In addition, the citizens of the United States, always an expansive and westward-looking people, were beginning to think in broad terms of the ultimate growth of their country from 13 Atlantic Coast colonies to a North American empire bounded to the west only by the Pacific.

So quickly and thoroughly were early English immigrants assimilated into the mainstream of American culture that it is now impossible to determine just how many Americans who came to Texas prior to its revolt against Mexico were native English. Certainly, however, a significant proportion of Austin's colonists were of English birth, as were those of a second successful American impresario, Green DeWitt, and when the Texas Revolution came in 1836 these men and women played a prominent role in the fight for freedom. Of the 187 Texans to die at the siege of the Alamo, 16 were Welsh or English.[1]

Valentine Bennet's family was of the minor aristocracy in the north of England but moved to the United States in time for him to fight against his home country in the War of 1812. Like many Americans of his day, Bennet found the East too confining and followed the frontier first to Louisiana, then to the Ohio Territory and finally to Brazoria in Austin's Texas colony. On June 26, 1831, Bennet became the first English Texan to shed his blood in the cause of Texan freedom when he was severely wounded in the storming of Fort Velasco, the first open armed defiance of the colonists against Mexico. Recovering from his wound, Bennet became one of the "immortal eighteen" in the "Come and Take It" fight at Gonzales and served as a lieutenant of Texas Volunteers at the battle of Concepción. During the siege of Bexar Bennet was promoted to the rank of major and appointed quartermaster of the Texas army. General Edward Burleson praised Bennet for "the diligence and success" with which he supplied the army, and it was Major Bennet who handed the axe to Deaf Smith with which the chief of scouts felled Vince's Bridge, a decisive event in the battle of San Jacinto.[2]

Charles Shearn, born in Bath in 1794, immigrated to Texas in 1834 and the next year became a signer of the Goliad Declaration of Independence. Shearn joined Colonel James Fannin's ill-fated army and was captured by the Mexicans but was spared his comrades' fate at Goliad because he was a British subject. Following the battle of San Jacinto, however, he became a citizen of the Republic of Texas and served as chief justice of the Harris County courts from 1837 to 1843.[3]

Another Englishman to barely escape death at Goliad was Joseph Lancaster. Born in Devonport in 1816, Lancaster was apprenticed to a printer until 1831 when he stowed away on a ship bound for New York. On his way west he worked on newspapers first in Kentucky and then in Alabama, where he joined the Red Rovers to fight for Texas's freedom. Acting as a courier between Colonel Fannin and General

Charles Shearn   *Thomas William House*

Houston, he was saved from capture and execution by a sympathetic Mexican woman. Thus Lancaster lived to fight at San Jacinto and eventually to return to Alabama to resume his career in journalism.[4]

John Hallett was born in Worcestershire, the younger son of an English nobleman. Commissioned into the Royal Navy at the age of 12, young Hallett deserted to an American ship and fought against the British in the War of 1812. Following the United States' second war with the mother country, Hallett left the sea, married and moved to Texas, settling first at Goliad but moving in 1833 to Austin's colony. There he homesteaded a site on the Lavaca River which was soon to become known as Hallettsville, the seat of Lavaca County. The old sailor died not long after his move to Austin's colony, but his oldest son, John Hallett Jr., fought under General Sam Houston at San Jacinto, the battle which won Texas independence.[5]

Perhaps the most notable of all Englishmen to establish their homes and loyalties with the frontier republic was Thomas William House of the English shire of Somerset. Born in 1814, House, much like John Hallett, ran away to sea at an early age but jumped ship in New York. There he served as a baker's apprentice until he was recruited by the world-famous St. Charles Hotel in New Orleans as a pastry chef.

Hallettsville

Austin home of Edward Mandell House

By 1836 House was establishing a solid reputation as a master chef in a city known for its culinary delights, when events beyond the Sabine seduced him away to a life of adventure.

After service under Burleson and Houston in the Texas Revolution, House remained in the new town of Houston where he reestablished his bakery business, acted as agent for British capitalists investing in Texas and soon expanded his bakery business into dry goods, wholesale groceries and cotton speculation. He bought plantations, ranches and wharves in Houston and Galveston, and by 1860 in all of Houston his personal fortune was exceeded only by that of William Marsh Rice. House is credited with producing and selling the first ice cream in Houston as well as with establishing that city's first bank. He served as Confederate mayor of Houston[6] and, perhaps most importantly, was father of Colonel Edward M. House, "kingmaker" of Texas Governor James S. Hogg and United States President Woodrow Wilson. Edward was considered "the Texas Talleyrand" at the Versailles Convention at the end of World War I.[7]

Edward Mandell House

Men of English birth fought side by side with their American-born cousins to make the independence of Texas a reality; English judicial tradition influenced the constitution of the new republic, based on United States statute and upon the laws of England as well. The Constitution of the Republic of Texas was a direct and lineal descendant of the Magna Carta, the Petition of Rights and the Bill of Rights, all of which had become part of the English law prior to 1700. The constitution written by the founders of the Texas republic in 1836 was built upon a framework of traditional Anglo-American ideas modified by the influences of Jacksonian democracy and by the traditions of Spanish law and custom. Specific provisions of the 17-point Declaration of Rights, for example, may be traced directly to sections of the Magna Carta defining and guaranteeing due process of law and limiting the power of the executive to suspend laws. The prohibition against the quartering of soldiers in private homes was derived from the English Bill of Rights.[8]

By and large, the English government was well disposed toward the new republic. Her Majesty's ministers plainly foresaw that Texas, as a predominantly agricultural country, would be a lucrative market for England's manufactured goods, while her production of raw materials, principally cotton, literally the fiber of British industry, was potentially immense.[9] And Texas, in dire economic straits, sorely needed English recognition and commerce. In 1838 President Mirabeau B. Lamar counseled Lord Palmerston's envoy, William Kennedy: "Tell your rulers to agree to a liberal treaty with Texas and she will pursue a commercial system by which trade will be freed from its shackles in the valley of the Mississippi, and the country beyond the Rio Grande."[10]

Nevertheless, several special interest groups in England opposed diplomatic recognition of the new sovereignty and even attempted to exert their influence with Parliament to induce British arms and economic might to force Texas back into the Mexican federation. English holders of Mexican bonds, for example, were especially concerned over an independent Texas. In 1836 Mexico was indebted to British subjects in the amount of approximately £30 million. This debt was secured by bonds pledging 45,000,000 acres of unoccupied Texas land. In case of default, the English landholders were to gain title to land in Texas commensurate with the amount of their loan. With the victory of the Texas army at San Jacinto, of course, all Mexican and hence British claims to Texas lands became instantly nullified. Any attempt by Mexico to alienate those acres specifically mortgaged to English capital and "any attempt at usurping them by a foreign power," the bondholders claimed, "imposed upon England, as a matter of mere attorney practice, the necessity of imposing a bar to such misappropriation."[11]

Not only would Mexico's ability to pay her British creditors be diminished by Texan independence, but also English capitalists worried that trade between Mexico and Great Britain might be disrupted. British commercial interests in Mexico were great, and trade between British and Mexican ports was of tremendous profit to English shipping interests. Fearful of the loss of commerce, even though mindful of the instability of Santa Anna's regime in Mexico City, certain factions of English merchants hoped for Mexico's "early reconquest of her truant province"[12] after the Texas Declaration of Independence on March 2, 1836.

Other Englishmen, concerned primarily with England's own colonial empire, urged that the crown refuse to recognize the sovereignty of Texas and that Lord Palmerston, Queen Victoria's Foreign Minister, dispatch a naval force to the Gulf to help Mexico recover her lost state. Texas's successful fight for independence, they argued, would set an intolerable precedent for other colonial states with a mind toward their own freedom. The Texas Revolution, according to one Tory propagandist, afforded "an example which other nations may follow to the prejudice of this great colonial empire" as well as "exposing to imminent hazard the important interests of our countrymen throughout Mexico."[13]

Also of great concern to the guardians of the British Empire was the weakening of Mexico as a foil to the power of and a check against the westward expansion of the United States. The British also feared that Texas might be annexed to the United States. The merger of the two republics would form a single nation which even the might of British arms and diplomacy could not rival on the North American continent. At a time when the United States was pressing its claim for sovereignty over the Oregon territory—jointly claimed by the British crown—some English diplomats insisted that their country must be "deeply interested in Mexico's welfare" because their own territory, Oregon, "was exposed to the same danger as that of Mexico, and from the same source." The responsibility of the British government must, therefore, be to aid Mexico to resist what many saw as an American expansionist plot. With Texas and Mexico reunited, they contended, Santa Anna's government "would have weighed in the scale as a counterpoise to the United States, in the full integrity of her strength, in place of being placed at her mercy."[14]

Finally, in addition to financial, diplomatic and strategic reasons why England should support Mexico's claim to sovereignty over Texas, came the humanitarian appeal. Because the Mexican constitution of 1824 had at least nominally outlawed slavery, English abolitionists saw the revolt in Texas as a major defeat for the cause of emancipation. England in 1836 was the unquestioned leader of a worldwide crusade to abolish the international slave trade. In 1807 the transportation of slaves in English ships had been prohibited, and at the Congress of Vienna in 1815 England had convinced the European powers to outlaw the trade in blacks as well. In 1833 all slaves within the British empire were emancipated with compensation to their owners. English abolitionists were therefore quite disturbed at the prospect of recognition of a new slave-holding nation which might not choose to abide by the articles of the Congress of Vienna. Slavery had never actually been discontinued or even strongly discouraged in the Mexican province of Texas, and, with independence, English humanitarians feared that the vigorous young republic would push its boundaries farther to the west, thereby opening new territory to the "peculiar institution."

Further, the English liberals were very concerned over the fate of the Indians of Texas. For hundreds of years the Apaches and the Comanches had effectively blocked most Spanish and Mexican colonization north of the Rio Bravo. Additionally, the Comanches and their Kiowa allies launched such punishing raids into Coahuila, Nuevo Leon and beyond that Federal authorities in Mexico City had allowed Stephen Austin's Anglo-Americans to enter Texas largely to serve as a buffer between themselves and the Indians. The colonists became so adept at Indian warfare that within ten years the Apaches and Comanches were checked, and the less warlike Karankawa and Tonkawa tribes were facing extermination. From across the thousands of miles of ocean, humanitarians in England saw only the brutality of the Americans and the approaching doom of the tribes, never the savagery and terror inflicted by the Indians on the white settlers along the Brazos, Trinity and Colorado rivers. To the English, a return to Mexican rule would bring justice to the Indians and peace to the border—a belief totally unsupported by history or by the ethic of the Mexicans, the Indians or the American Texans. Thus, wrote one English supporter of Mexico's Texas claims, a successful reinvasion of the breakaway province

ought to be hailed with joy by every British subject—
the British creditors of Mexico would be restored to

their territorial rights—the British merchant would find a country cleared of cheats, rogues, and vagabonds . . . and well supplied with a metallic currency—the British philanthropist would see slavery abolished in Texas, and the remnants of ancient nations of *red men* preserved from extinction under the joint protection of Mexico and Great Britain.[15]

Happily for the new government of Texas, neither Lord Palmerston nor the majority of his advisors were of this mind. More common in northern and western Europe was the belief, as stated by Austrian novelist Charles Sealsfield, that the Texans were perfectly right in seceding from Mexico, for what Nordic people could bear being ruled by "bigoted, idle and ignorant peons" who were "both morally and physically inferior to themselves." A war against such people, he argued, "was no war at all," for a brigade of Anglo-American Texans could easily defeat a whole army of the "pigmy, spindle-shanked" Mexicans, "none of them so big or half as strong as American boys of fifteen."[16]

Such blatant ethnic prejudice was hardly unfamiliar to 19th century Europe, and despite the highly vocal minority of abolitionists and other humanitarians in England, the general consensus with regard to Texas's liberty was largely in line with Sealsfield's opinion. G.W. Featherstonhaugh, author of *Excursions through the Slave States*, for example, stated that "as Mexico is essentially a revolutionary government, and as no party at the capital will probably for a long time be strong enough to do more than attend to its own interests, it is almost self-evident that if ever she has the inclination, she will never have the power to govern—at a distance of 1,800 miles—a race of active and intrepid men, who are hostile to her laws, religion, and manners."[17] More succinctly, Francis C. Sheridan, grandson of the famous Irish playwright, Richard B. Sheridan, rebutted the argument that the Americans had "stolen" Texas from Mexico with the declaration that "if it were theft, it was a compulsory one."[18]

Arguments for England's recognition of Texas independence were, to Englishmen in general and eventually to Lord Palmerston, more convincing than the arguments against recognition. Francis Sheridan's perception of a potential Anglo-Texan alliance, for example, was most compelling if none too complimentary to the Texans. "If the recognition of this republic was ceded by Great Britain & emigration there encouraged & protected," he maintained, "Texas w[oul]d become comparatively speaking anglicised. The natural vanity inherent in Americans w[oul]d be greatly tickled by treating their brethren of the States with indifference, — bragging of their intercourse with England and Englishmen — & alluding at their Banquet speeches & Congress orations to the amicable feeling existing between the two countries."[19]

The struggle between the two factions, however, was a long and bitter one, hotly contested for four years. As early as the spring of 1837 Great Britain had sent William Kennedy as an unofficial representative of the consular service to Texas in order to assess the new country's viability as a permanent figure upon the world's stage and England's own best course of action toward it. So impressed with Texas's promise and vitality was the diplomat that he personally invested in a league of Texas land.[20] His favorable report, however, did not rush Palmerston's ministry into full diplomatic relations with Texas.

In an attempt to woo English attention, President Houston appointed former North Carolina aristocrat, Texas general and secretary of state, and future governor James Pinckney Henderson as agent to France and England. Henderson arrived in London in October 1837, to find considerable interest in his cause already current in England. The closely related factors of commercial benefit and political counterweight to growing American influence indicated to the Texas agent some willingness on the part of Great Britain to recognize his government.

James P. Henderson

Slavery and the slave trade remained, however, as a substantial barrier to Texas recognition. Soon after his arrival in London Henderson obtained an audience with Palmerston, at which time the Texas agent staunchly championed Britain's efforts at stamping out the international slave trade. He stated in the strongest terms his own government's position opposing the kidnapping and sale of Africans in their own land and its view of the transatlantic trade in Negroes as an act of piracy. The continuation of chattel slavery in Texas and the importation of blacks from the United States, however, were institutions which Texans were not willing to forego. Palmerston was impressed by Henderson's presentation and held out some hope of a treaty of commerce with Texas, if not full diplomatic recognition. Palmerston, accordingly, presented Henderson's petition to the British cabinet on December 27, only to see it flatly denied.

Disappointed but undaunted, Henderson took another tack. If Her Majesty's government would not open trade with Texas by treaty, might it not be possible to do so by simple agreement, he asked Palmerston. Such an agreement, while not binding England officially to recognition, would serve the same purpose to the infinite relief of the beleaguered republic. In practice, ships flying the Lone Star flag would be welcome in English ports and their cargoes cleared through customs as were those of officially recognized nations. Although England would still consider Texas a province of Mexico, Henderson proposed, British port officials could "shut their eyes to the circumstances of [ships] having Texan papers." Reciprocally, English ships would be welcomed to Texas ports, an arrangement which Henderson hoped would both revive the languishing Texas economy and increase English awareness of and respect for the Lone Star Republic.

Lord Palmerston rightly considered the proposal somewhat unusual, but at last gave it his blessing and sent it along to the Board of Trade which approved it in April. The Texas government, of course, quickly ratified the agreement, and President Houston signed it into law on July 4, 1838. The quasi recognition of Texas by the world's preeminent power was, for the struggling young republic, a diplomatic triumph of the first order.[21]

Texans were soon drinking to "The health of the youthful Sovereign of the British Empire!" and referring to Queen Victoria's nation as their "grandmother country." Many a distinguished after-dinner speaker, Kennedy reported, looked eagerly forward to England's full

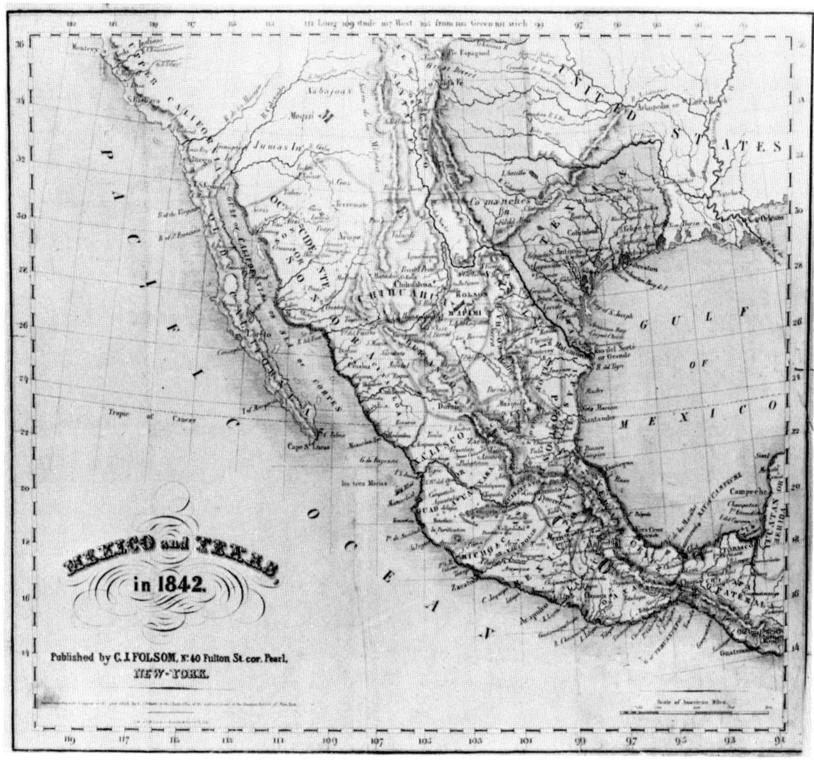

and complete "recognition of the right which patriotism had established by an untarnished sword," which would admit Texas to the family of nations in legal as well as commercial fact.[22]

Her Majesty's government was willing to grant Texas full diplomatic recognition if such recognition did not impair England's favorable financial and diplomatic relations with Mexico. As a condition of such recognition, England wished first to see a treaty of peace agreed to between Mexico and her former province and Mexico's explicit recognition of Texas's independence. England, however, was willing to use its economic and diplomatic might to secure such an agreement on Texas's behalf. To this end Sir Richard Packenham, the British ambassador to Mexico, offered his good offices as negotiator between Mexico and Texas. As the question of Mexican bonds for Texas territory held by British subjects continued to be a sticking point in Anglo-Texan negotiations, and as the Texas government was willing to pay Mexico $5 million to establish a permanent peaceful border at the Rio Grande, the wily

Packenham perceived a means by which all three parties to the negotiations might come out winners.

If British bondholders would accept $5 million in Texas lands (the very lands by which the bonds had originally been secured), and if Mexico would accept Texas cash, English investors would drop their opposition to Texas freedom, Mexico's financially embarrassed government would be enriched by $5 million, and Texas would gain legal as well as *de facto* status as an independent nation and a stable and secure southern border, as well as England's full diplomatic recognition. The arrangement would cost Texas $5 million in cash and $5 million in land; Mexico would give up only its unenforceable claim to an ungovernable northern province, and Great Britain would lose nothing.[23]

England's offer was unhesitatingly declined by Mexican authorities, and each wind from the west blew reports of renewed hostilities along the Rio Grande into the port of London. James Hamilton, Texas's bond salesman in England, wrote home in April 1840 that "every false rumor of Mexican and Indian invasion brings us to a standstill." All such rumors of war were not precipitated by Mexican hostilities, for Texans were tired of the perpetual guerrilla warfare waged along their southern border and their status of unrecognized sovereignty. The war party in Austin was clamoring for an incursion into Mexico to end once and for all this state of limbo, but the Texas agent in London warned that "a premature invasion of Mexico would dash our well-digested schemes to the ground, and subvert, in one hour, my incessant and irksome labor for the last eighteen months."[24]

Apparently heeding his plea, Hamilton's fellow Texans refrained from a rash move against Mexico, thus increasing Texas's esteem in the eyes of the world community and strengthening its agent's diplomatic hand in London. In October Hamilton submitted to Lord Palmerston a rough draft of a treaty of recognition and commerce, and finally, despite some last-ditch delays by the English pro-Mexican faction, the first of three treaties was signed by Her Majesty's government. This treaty was quickly followed by a second promising English mediation between Mexico and Texas, and a third pledging Texas's support of the suppression of the slave trade. These treaties were speedily ratified by the Texas Legislature, and although the Mexican government signaled its scorn of the agreements by sending General Adrian Woll across the Rio Grande to temporarily reoccupy San Antonio, they represented the greatest international diplomatic achievement of the Texas republic.

Thanks to the goodwill of England, Texas statesmanship assured in the Court of St. James the liberty that Texas arms had won on the field of San Jacinto.[25]

This new phase in Anglo-Texan relations was inaugurated by the arrival in Galveston in the summer of 1842 of England's first chargé d'affaires and consul general in Texas, a remarkable young officer of the Royal Navy named Charles Elliot. A man "blessed with aristocracy of talent and birth" and possessed of "intense experience and forceful reactions," Captain Elliot was destined to play a major role in the political and diplomatic history of the Texas republic. Lord Aberdeen, Palmerston's successor as foreign secretary, instructed Elliot to collect and transmit to the foreign office "Information upon all matters of political Interest and importance," and the chargé lost no opportunity to enlighten his superiors in England about conditions in Texas. From a general lack of interest in 1841, England was converted through Captain Elliot's letters to a position of utmost concern with happenings in Texas and consequently of vigorous diplomatic and commercial activity there.[26]

Captain Charles Elliot

A political dreamer, a sincere philanthropist and yet a strong English patriot, the new chargé committed the next four years to establishing a lasting peace between Mexico and her former northernmost state, Texas independence from both Mexican and United States' sovereignty, and the abolition of slavery within the boundaries of the republic. Elliot quickly arrived at the conclusion that Mexico lacked the strength ever to reconquer her breakaway province and that her "predatory" raids into Texas were actually counterproductive. They accomplished nothing of positive value and only irritated allies and enemies alike. Although the chargé informed Aberdeen that "when the Character of the Mexican Government and people is considered," it would seem that reason "would have long since made it a matter of indifference to Texas whether Mexico acknowledge its independence or not," Elliot threw himself into the diplomatic struggle to put a stop to the "fruitless and desultory" war which still existed between Mexico and Texas.[27]

Humanitarianism was not Elliot's sole motivation. Although England never desired to annex Texas herself, as was greatly feared in the United States, she was most anxious to prevent such an annexation by the United States. Thus Her Majesty's foreign office did its utmost during 1843-1845 to induce Mexico to recognize Texas independence, hoping thereby to lessen the desire of Texans for annexation. Besides wishing to see a strong independent Texas as a blockade to U.S. expansion to the west, Englishmen such as Charles Elliot envisioned the emancipation of slavery in the Texas republic and, from that beginning, the ultimate destruction of chattel slavery on the North American continent. Although Captain Elliot truthfully reported to London that Texas slaves were seldom ill-fed or ill-used by their masters, he proposed that Britain advance a loan to Texas with which to purchase and emancipate slaves in Texas. In return for emancipation, Her Majesty's government would exert pressure on Mexico to recognize Texas independence, applying the argument that "the abolition of Slavery in Texas would . . . be a greater triumph, and more honourable to Mexico, than the retention of any sovereignty merely nominal." With free labor established in Texas, Elliot believed, "what with the opportunity of procuring labor from Mexico," Texas would soon outstrip the states of the Deep South in the production of cotton. Thus the raising of that staple and the keeping of the slaves who nurtured it would become unprofitable, and the institution would die out.[28]

The sudden gust of interest in Texas from London roused the United States. In his annual message to Congress in 1842, President John Tyler issued a warning to England to keep her hands off of both Texas and Oregon. Secretary of State Daniel Webster was convinced that "a European power" was seeking to gain control over Texas and damage American interests there, and Andrew Jackson feared that Texas might become "worse than a colony of England, involved in constant conflict with the United States." John C. Calhoun, the foremost spokesman for the cotton states, felt that Texas had been "invaded" by "British gold" and by "interested and wily diplomacy," and that of all possible diplomatic crises, an Anglo-Texan alliance "would be the most disastrous." Presidential aspirant James K. Polk believed "in truth and in fact" that Great Britain intended to make Texas "a dependency of her own."[29]

President Houston shrewdly played both English and American fears to Texas's advantage. To Charles Elliot he confided that to defuse the threat of U.S. annexation, it was "only necessary for Lord Aberdeen to say to Santa Anna, 'Sir, Mexico must recognize the independence of Texas!' and thus obviate the necessity of protection by the U.S." "Her Majesty's Govt. might rest assured," Elliot reported to Aberdeen, that with Texas independence recognized by Mexico, President Houston "would never consent to any treaty on this project of annexation to the United States."[30]

London, 1840

To the United States, however, the Houston administration hinted darkly that if Texas's safety were not guaranteed by immediate annexation, the infant republic must look across the Atlantic for protection from Mexico. Thus, on April 22, 1844, President Tyler was moved to send an annexation treaty to the Senate "to further the mutual security and prosperity of the United States and Texas." If annexation failed, Tyler told the Senate, Texas would surely seek friendship elsewhere.[31]

Charles Elliot was vastly relieved to learn that on June 8 the Senate, largely because of the slavery issue, had defeated annexation by a sizeable margin. The foreign office quickly heightened its efforts to draw Texas closer to England and drive a wedge between the two banks of the Sabine. Aberdeen advised Texans that "the dignity and prosperity" of their country "are more secure in its own keeping than under the institutions of any other government, however peaceful. . . . It must be long," he counseled, "before a newly settled and comparatively thinly peopled country would command the attention and the weight which would make up for the abandonment of the privilege of self-government—if indeed such a result should ever be attainable." He also urged France to join England in exerting pressure on Mexico to recognize Texas's freedom and cease her attacks across the Rio Grande. So great were Elliot's personal efforts to keep Texas out of the Union that he later drew President Polk's rebuke for "open intermeddling" in Texas policy. Despite the best efforts of her diplomats, however, England failed to sway Mexico from its anti-Texas policy, and on February 28, 1845, Congress passed a joint resolution which President Tyler signed the following day, offering statehood to the Lone Star Republic.[32]

Once spurned, Texans were less eager than they had been a year earlier for annexation. Many influential Texans—Elliot's close friends Anson Jones, the new president of the republic, and Ashbel Smith, its secretary of state, foremost among them—advocated Texas's continued independence if peace with Mexico could be secured. Toward that end, Elliot, Jones, Smith and the French chargé, Count Alphonse de Saligny, prepared an ultimatum-memorandum for presentation to the Mexican authorities. In return for Mexico's acknowledgment of Texas independence, the young republic offered its pledge never to allow itself to be annexed by the United States.

In secret and with great haste Captain Elliot personally carried the proposal to Mexico. Sailing out of Galveston on March 29, 1845, Elliot landed at Veracruz and made his way overland to Mexico City, racing against the day the Texas voters would ratify annexation. Despite being robbed on the road to the Mexican capital, Elliot presented the Texas proposition to Minister of Foreign Affairs Luis G. Cuevas, who, after frustrating delays, on May 17 signed the document which at last assured peace and freedom for Texas.[33]

Elliot sped back to Washington-on-the-Brazos with news of his greatest diplomatic triumph, only to have his enthusiasm dashed by President Jones's assessment of Texas's political situation. In Elliot's absence, he said, public opinion had swung around to almost unanimous support for union with the United States, and no treaty with Mexico could turn that tide. Despite high praise from Lord Aberdeen for "dexterity and activity" while serving as chargé, all three of Charles Elliot's great dreams were shattered. On July 4, 1845, a Texas convention voted for annexation; Texas legally entered the Union on December 29, 1845, although transfer of authority from the republic to the state did not take place until February 19, 1846. Three months later, largely in reaction to the treaty of annexation, full-scale war broke out along the Rio Grande between the United States and Mexico. With the formalities of annexation complete, Charles Elliot closed the offices of Her Majesty's consulate in Texas and returned to London.[34] As he sailed home across the Atlantic, his dreams in tatters, he passed hundreds of his countrymen bound for Texas with visions of a new and better life in a great new territory.

Chapter 2
Colonial Enterprise—
The Immigrants

Besides Charles Elliot, two other British subjects sojourning in Texas during the epoch of the republic were destined to leave their imprint upon Texas diplomatic history: Arthur Ikin and William Kennedy. Ikin first came to Texas in January 1841, bearing the commercial treaties negotiated between Palmerston's foreign ministry and the Sam Houston administration. So impressed was the president by the English envoy that on February 4 he returned Ikin to London as consul for the Republic of Texas. While in this capacity, Ikin published *Texas: Its History, Topography, Agriculture, Commerce, and General Statistics,* a volume highly laudatory of the newly recognized republic.[1]

William Kennedy first traveled in Texas in 1839 as secretary to the Earl of Durham. In the same year that Ikin's book appeared, Kennedy published *The Rise, Progress, and Prospects of Texas* which also presented the country in the finest light and encouraged British immigration to Texas. In 1842 he replaced Ikin as Texas consul in London and later in that year was returned to Texas as British consul in Galveston.[2]

Not only were Ikin and Kennedy of service to the Republic as diplomats and as propagandists of the Texas cause, but both men greatly encouraged their countrymen to immigrate to Texas, and both attempted to found English colonies there.

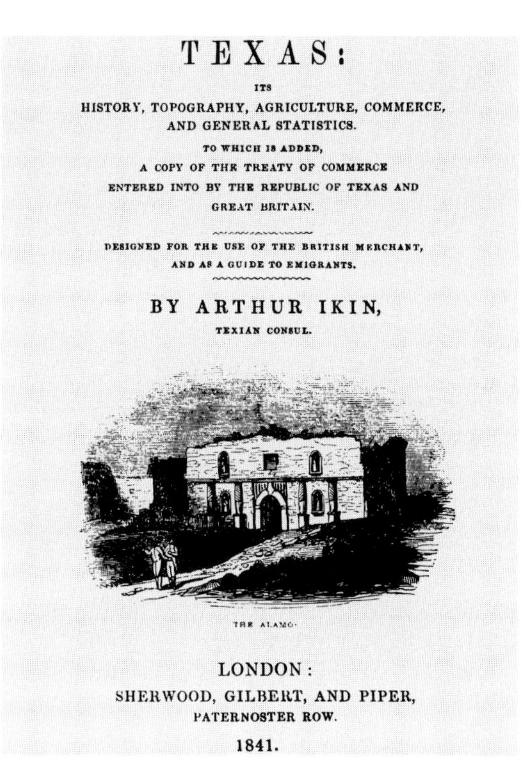

In 1836 Arthur Ikin's father, Jonathan, had purchased a tract of Texas land from Judge John Woodward, the Texas consul in New York. Realizing that British recognition of Texas independence would enhance the value of their lands, the Ikins spent years working toward that end. With the eventual English recognition of Texas, the first of a planned series of colonial immigration groups sailed from London for the Ikin holdings. Landing at Galveston in the winter of 1839-1840, they learned to their dismay that they "had not a shadow of a title" to the lands which Arthur and Jonathan Ikin had supposedly sold to them. The swindler, in this case, had been Judge Woodward, and the Ikins were quickly absolved of any charge of evildoing. The problem of a shipload of settlers stranded in Galveston remained, however, so in June 1840 Jonathan Ikin applied to President Lamar for a tract of public land on which to settle his English colonists. Due largely to their work toward British recognition, the Ikins were granted a colonization contract by the republic, and Arthur resumed his role as "chief land salesman and leading emigration advocate for Texas."[3]

Unfortunately for these indefatigable propagandists of the Texas cause, their colonization scheme was ultimately a failure. The next group of Ikin colonists were to have left England in June 1842, but balked at news of renewed warfare on the Rio Grande and rumors of an imminent Mexican invasion. The Ikins' attempts to settle Texas with English immigrants ended with this failure, and neither lived to reap the financial benefit of their efforts on behalf of the republic or to see the land that they had been granted fill with prosperous farms and ranches.

Also in 1842 William Kennedy obtained a contract to settle 600 English families south of the Nueces River, but the proposed colony came to naught.

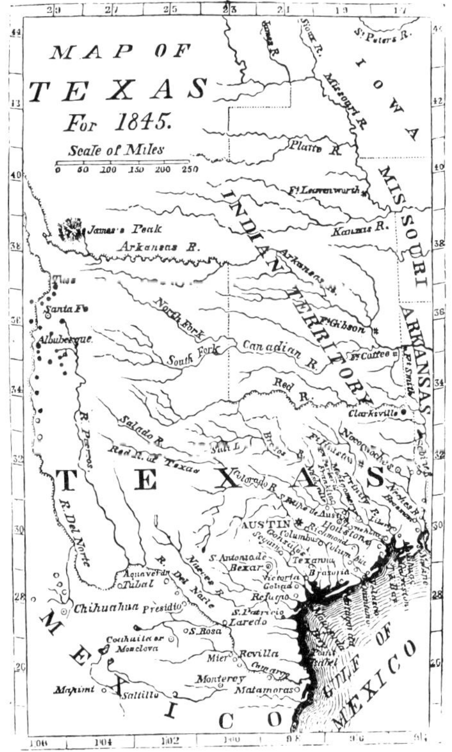

By the mid-19th century many Englishmen were as convinced of America's future prosperity as was Captain J. Bertie Cator of the Royal Navy who told his sons that the United States "will be one of these days the most wealthy place in the world. England will be past living in for a poor man."[4] And no section of the American continent was more loudly praised than was the Republic and later the State of Texas. Typical of the English newspaper response to Texas's prospects is this item from the *Times* of London:

> Few countries present so many attractions to emigrants,
> and if they do not prosper they would fail anywhere.
> Splendid arable and grazing lands may be purchased
> at merely nominal prices; labor is in demand and highly
> paid, living is inexpensive, and there are openings on
> all sides for the profitable investment of capital.

Land speculators contributed to the general enthusiasm for Texas, for example, Arthur Ikin with his incandescent evaluation of the republic's "milder climate and more fertile soil" and the inducement of "the British language, religion, and common law, as well as the attraction of free institutions and low taxation; to which may be added, a less complicated political, and a more liberal commercial system."[5]

Disinterested English travelers, too, returned with extravagant praise for Texas's resources. Matilda Charlotte Houstoun, for example, told her English readers that "it cannot be denied, that as a field for settlers, Texas has considerable advantages over almost every other country. Its climate . . . is excellent, and the settler has to encounter neither the extreme cold of the winter season, nor the scorching summer heat of the more northern states of America and Canada." This world traveler and journalist told the readers of the London *News* that she could "but regret that some thousands of our starving population cannot be conveyed to this country," for although the colonization of Australia and New Zealand were no doubt advantageous to Great Britain, the same good fortune seldom attended the poor colonist.[6]

Steamship and railroad companies as well as colonization enterprises aided the immigration effort. The railroads of Texas each contributed to an advertising agency $25.00 for each mile of track they operated to help support the propaganda machine which they had established in Europe.[7]

So great was the English interest in Texas and the American West that Robert Montgomery Bird's *Nick of the Woods*, an 1837 novel of Indian fighting on the American frontier, quickly went through nine English editions. English writers, seeing a profitable market, soon began producing imitations of the American "Western" with Percy St. John and Mayne Reid among the most successful writers of the genre. Reid, in fact, published more than 70 novels of the American West, each plentifully spiced with violence and high adventure. As Ray Allen Billington pointed out, "these best-sellers played a larger role than any other writings in shaping the European image of the American frontier."[8]

A great deal of money and effort were invested in making the Englishman aware of Texas in the mid-19th century and in interesting him in immigrating to this largely wild and unsettled place. All such efforts, however, would probably have failed had conditions then existing in the old country not generated a restlessness in its population and predisposed a large segment of its young men and women toward casting their lot in a new and strange land. To a people overburdened by tithes, taxes and landlords, and too often crowded into smoky industrial slums, the promise of abundant, cheap and fertile land was exciting beyond description. Although few fled outright starvation at home, almost none who came to Texas failed to vastly improve their social and economic station in life. The greatest number of English immigrants to Texas had been farmers in Great Britain, where the average farm consisted of one to ten acres. A 40- to 60-acre plot in Europe was considered huge, while in Texas a whole 640-acre section of undeveloped prairie land was to be had for as little as $5.00.

Not only English ploughmen and husbandmen were drawn to the bright dream of owning a farm of their own. For quite a large number of mechanics and factory workers, land on the Texas frontier was a safety valve against urban and industrial discontent,[9] and even among the landed gentry a farm in Texas was a pleasing solution to the problem of the second or third son with no prospect of inheriting a piece of the ancestral domain. Under the English law of primogeniture the eldest son is entitled to the exclusive right of inheritance of all of his parents' real estate. Although this system held together the ancestral domains of the English aristocracy and provided social and economic stability from generation to generation, it also considerably reduced the prospects of all female and younger male descendants. Primogeniture was quickly abandoned in America's more democratic environment, and at least one Englishman in Texas wondered "where the English got their notion that the eldest son or daughter were more important than any of the other children." Lillie Barr Munroe knew several young men in Austin during the 1850's, "younger sons of great families, as fine men as could be," whom she felt to be virtually exiled to the New World. Such an arrangement was, to her mind, "silly stuff" and entirely "outside justice."[10]

Unfortunately for the English agriculturist and mechanic, Texas was too often oversold by enthusiastic land speculators. The avarice of unscrupulous land agents coupled with the naive expectations of British emigrants made hardships and failures among those who made the long trip from England almost inevitable.[11] William Kennedy's declaration that Texas's "black waxy soil" covered the surface to a depth of 20 feet with "nothing like a hillock or stone to bother the plowman," surely was stuff of much bitter reflection by Englishmen who had acquired poor Texas land, and the paeans to Texas's natural beauty sung by Dr. Edward Smith, an English traveler in Texas in 1849, were yet more fanciful. Smith chanted the praises of "the twining of beautiful cactus" and noted that even the "dreaded rattler and moccasin snakes have most beautifully painted skins, and the tarantula, to my eye, an elegant form and color." This intoxicated wanderer even paid homage to the "green headed prairie fly" and admired the "unsurpassed . . . lightness and elegance of form" of the mosquito![12] Fraudulent land salesmen circulated throughout England, selling titles to nonexistent or already owned acreage, while others grossly misrepresented the quality of their offerings. Ignorant of speculators' guile, many British settlers were sold land advertised as arable, only to arrive in Texas and find that their freehold was, in fact, nothing but poor grazing country.

Although many land companies advertised only for agriculturists and even went so far as to warn tradesmen not to leave England, many city-dwellers deliberately fled from the industrialization going on around them in an attempt to return to an older, simpler way of life.[13] "In those days it was generally supposed that any man could naturally farm, just as it was expected that every girl naturally knew how to cook and clean house," commented one English immigrant.[14] Too often these urban-bred agrarians failed to recognize the sacrifices in standard of living that frontier existence demanded.[15] Since cheap land was Texas's main attraction to British settlers, many did not select their farmsteads with great wisdom, either with respect to its potential for raising profitable crops or as a suitable location for carrying on a civilized social life.[16]

Especially demoralized by the hardships of the passage and the want of social amenities in the new land were the women of the "better" English classes. Isabel Holdsworth, recounting the story of her family's move from England to Frio County when she was a young girl, describes her father as "an adventurous spirit" who "having heard of the wonderful opportunities for acquiring land in the practically unsettled state of

Emigrants at dinner on shipboard

Texas . . . determined to give up his profession, dispose of his property in England, and risk his fortune in a new country."[17]

The weather was stormy in crossing the Atlantic, and the mother of the family was continually seasick. Her three children looked after themselves, ordered their own meals and "enjoyed the novelty of our experience." The arrival in Texas was more auspicious, for the newcomers believed in that spring "Texas had put on her most inviting aspect to impress her new settlers with their good fortune!" Their road from Galveston to the village of Derby cut through vast fields of wildflowers, but on arriving at their destination the mother experienced a feeling of utter abandonment. Although the children "ran merrily about, pouncing on flower after flower," Mrs. Holdsworth "felt both apprehensive and forlorn" as she sat amid her baggage and wondered what was to be their fate in the new country.[18]

Many frontier wives had attended finishing schools in England and had led sheltered lives before coming to Texas. Unaccustomed to manual labor and highly conscious of social status, these immigrant women generally made poor pioneers. Worst of all for them was the deprivation of friendship. "By far the severest burden" of frontier existence, wrote one middle-class English lady, was that "I had no friends with feeling like my own, no brother or Sister to whom I could speak of my heart sickness, my pains and fears."[19]

Nevertheless, the majority of the English settlers, perhaps because they had invested their all in their new land and had no recourse but to stay, persevered. "Notwithstanding the fact that my mother had never done any household work and had been accustomed to the comforts and conveniences of civilization," continues Isabel Holdsworth, "she now lived in a tent and learned to cook over a campfire." Her father, too, who had been a schoolmaster in England and "who had been unused to any form of mannual labor" soon became inured to the rough work of farm and ranch.[20]

Isabel Holdsworth's family was by no means exceptional in its exposure to "tarantulas, scorpions and snakes." Typical also were the great distances which they had to travel for lumber, drinking water and companionship. The sense of isolation was deadly, with the nearest neighbor four miles distant, the mail service irregular at best, and school- ing all but nonexistent. Other English immigrants recall having to haul water to the Panhandle or purchase it at 25¢ per barrel,[21] living below ground in dugouts for their first years in Texas, experiencing winters so severe that families had to stack their furniture on one side of their house and move their horses in with them to keep the valuable beasts from freezing.[22] Disease, too, was a great hazard to immigrant families on the frontier. Malaria, cholera and typhoid were especially endemic to Texas, and even when not fatal, an attack of one of these dreaded plagues could debilitate the victim for years.[23] Holidays were especially depressing to many newcomers, for recollections of festive occasions in the old country made the isolation of the new harder to bear. "On Christmas day," one English rancher lamented, "no Mexican can be got to work for love or money, so the fiesta, as they call it, was kept as best we might in that out-of-the-way place; not without memories of other Christmas days, so different from these, and distant friends, and holly-decked churches in far-off England."[24]

One old-time resident of Wharton County remembered that "many first-class English families came here, and when they found we had mass only once in four Sundays, they left."[25] But others, made of sterner stuff, shared the determination of the English pioneer who told a San Antonio newspaper reporter that "we were told when we came here that we would not live in Philadelphia."[26] Those who stayed helped to bring Texas to its present greatness; those who returned to England attempted to warn their countrymen of the perils awaiting the unprepared. In 1842 *The Emigration Gazette and Colonial Advocate* ran the following caveat:

> The writer of the CAUTION TO THE PUBLIC is one of three survivors out of ninety-seven Englishmen who were induced to emigrate to the inhospitable swamps called Texas in 1841. To detail the misery and hardships that the present writer and his deluded associates were exposed to on their arrival in the country, and the CERTAIN SICKNESS IF NOT DEATH that awaits those who may be tempted to emigrate to that land of fevers and disease of all kinds, would be quite impossible within the limits of this caution; which is meant simply to warn the working class against the manifold schemes now put forth by a base set of YANKEE TEXAS LAND SHARKS, to delude them.[27]

As late as 1879 the London *Standard* continued to warn its readers that those who had recently immigrated had been "deceived" and that Texas "is unfitted for English settlers of the better class." Nevertheless, distaste for commercial life, desire for independence, love of leisure, faith in subsistence farming or a taste for adventure continued throughout the 19th century to draw English craftsmen, domestic workers, farmers, merchants and professional people to Texas in appreciable numbers.[28]

The exodus of the English to North America was by no means a new thing in the mid-19th century. Between 1628 and 1642, 80,000 British, fully 2 percent of the total population of England and Wales, departed Great Britain; 58,000 came to America. Although "the great migration" diminished considerably during the 18th century, by the end of the colonial period 60 percent of all Americans were of English birth or descent. In the decades immediately following the American Revolution, English immigration to the United States slowed to a trickle, but in the second quarter of the 19th century, 410,000 English and Welsh sailed to America. The second half of the century brought 631,000 additional British to these shores. Of this last group, however, only 6 percent settled in the South and Southwest.[29]

The earliest English arrivals in Texas were often repulsed by the climate, the conditions of pioneer life and the potentially deadly tension between Texas and the Mexican republic. Not until after the United

The last day in Old England

States' war with Mexico, ending in 1848, did Texas become attractive to large numbers of English emigrants.[30] In 1860 the total native English population of San Antonio, Galveston, Houston, Austin and New Braunfels, then the principal Texas towns, was only 249 as compared to 282 Irish, 587 Mexican and 2,936 German natives.[31] The next 20 years added but 155 new British families to this sum from a total of 31,907 immigrant families of all nations.[32] The years between 1850 and 1890 saw a rise of native English living in the Plains states west of the Mississippi from 3 to 11 percent of all English in America. Most of these immigrants were in the Midwest because as of 1890 no county in Texas boasted even as many as 1,000 English- or Welsh-born citizens.[33]

As a means of populating the vast and vacant expanses of Texas, the Mexican government had adopted the expedient of granting impresario contracts to prominent or merely ambitious applicants. The impresario was deeded large tracts of unsettled land on which he pledged to settle a fixed number of families. The government of the Republic of Texas at first renounced, but later reinstated the impresario system. Before Texas gained its independence, however, several English gentlemen had procured Mexican impresario grants in Texas, and some patents granted prior to the revolution were revoked by the new republic. In the words of one historian of the European settlement of North America, "for magnitude and magnificence of speculative projects, for diversity and flamboyance of salesmanship, and for colorful and controversial opinions, Texas had no peers."[34] Nonetheless, several colonial enterprises were conceived and attempted in hopes of making Texas a "young England." Unfortunately for planners and colonists alike, none of these were successful, and some were tragic failures.[35]

Major General Arthur G. Wavell, an English army officer, attempted the first program of colonizing Texas with British farmers in the 1820's. Wavell was in Mexico City as early as 1821 working for the Mexican government.[36] There he met and befriended Stephen F. Austin who was seeking Texas lands and permission to settle English-speaking immigrants on them. The English soldier, whose knowledge of the Spanish language and Mexican administrative procedure far exceeded that of Austin, was able to render the prospective American colonizer considerable assistance, and Wavell and Austin struck an agreement to form a joint stock company to help develop Austin's grant. The company never materialized, but Wavell, fired by Austin's success, petitioned the Mexican government for a tract in northeast Texas to which he promised to bring 450 British Catholics. Wavell secured official approval for his scheme on March 9, 1826, and hired his close friend, Benjamin Milam, to serve as the proposed colony's resident manager.[37]

Wavell raised $2,000 in English capital to finance his project and, with Milam's assistance, located hundreds of families on the grant, although few of these were British as planned. With Milam's heroic death at the siege of Bexar in 1835, the colony began to wither, and, with Texas independence, the legality of the claim was called into question. Wavell petitioned the republic, reminding it that but for his aid "Austin certainly, and probably Milam, the martyr of your cause, would have forever abandoned Texas," and asked that his grant be recognized by the new government.[38] The republic, however, voided Wavell's Mexican impresario contracts, and the colony soon fell apart. "Conceived by a soldier of fortune, supported by a reckless adventurer, and designed to transport independent-minded English-speaking Britons into a government-restricted, Spanish-speaking territory," one historian of Texas colonization has noted, "the first major attempt to promote British emigration to Texas quite naturally failed."[39]

Although the war for Texas independence frustrated any colonizing attempt during the mid-1830's, by the beginning of the new decade several English companies were preparing to move colonists to their New World holdings.[40] William S. Peters, his three sons-in-law and 16 other associates, about half of whom were English and the remainder

William S. Peters

American, secured in 1841 a grant of land extending south from the Red River into present-day Cooke, Denton, Grayson and Collin counties. In return the Peters Company was to locate 600 families on the grant within three years. In November the grant was extended to include parts of Tarrant, Dallas, Ellis and Johnson counties with the promise of 200 additional families. In July of 1842 a ten-mile strip was added to the western and a twelve-mile strip to the eastern boundaries of the grant, and the three-year time limit was pushed back to date from the acquisition of the newest lands. Finally, on January 16, 1843, the grant was extended to a princely 16,000 square miles with five years given to the company to find and relocate settlers. Further evidence of the brilliant salesmanship of the Peters Company or the extreme naivete of the Texas Legislature is to be found in the republic's proviso that "the grantees would limit themselves to the introduction of not more than 10,000 families!"[41]

Peters and his associates, incorporated in London as the Texas Agricultural, Commercial, and Manufacturing Company, now began to turn their attention to populating their vast new holdings. Newspaper advertisements and pamphlets began to appear all over England promising great rewards to the potential emigrant. An agent of the company would meet migrant parties at Galveston or New Orleans and guide them to their new homes along the Red River. Comfortable housing was to be built by the company and provided to the settlers immediately upon their arrival. Food, fuel and clothing were to be supplied to the colonists until their first crop was harvested, and in addition to the 160 to 240 acres promised to each family, each group of 100 families would receive 1,280 acres for religious and educational purposes. All of the largess, including transportation to Texas, would cost the colonist £50 per adult and an additional £12 for each child. The settler also pledged to live on his land for at least three years and to fence and cultivate at least 15 acres.[42]

Those Englishmen unfortunate enough to have taken the company at its word found conditions in Texas considerably short of those promised by Peters and his associates. With all food imported to the colony at tremendous expense across hundreds of miles of hostile Indian territory, "many died of starvation, whilst placed in one of the most fertile spots under the sun." Under these circumstances, reported Edward Smith, scout for the Universal Emigration and Colonization Company, another English company also looking to colonial enterprise in northeast Texas, "many Europeans emigrated to that part of the

Henry Oliver Hedgcoxe, agent for the Peters Company

country, and died there; or returned to their former homes, disgusted with the dangers and privations of Texas."[43]

Despite the wonderful incentives, very few Englishmen accepted the Texas Agricultural, Commercial, and Manufacturing Company's offer, and by 1848 only 2.3 percent of the colony's inhabitants were European-born, and the majority of those who were had previously lived in the United States. By 1844 the colony had been divided between two rival factions of the company, one of which survived only because of an influx of American settlers from the eastern states and the other of which failed absolutely with its lands reverting to Texas for breach of contract.[44]

Even with the lessons of Wavell, Peters and several similar failures before them, one more British company made the grandest attempt of all to establish a piece of England on Texas soil, and its failure was the most spectacular of all. The Universal Emigration and Colonization Company was the brainchild of a man otherwise lost to history, known only as Mr. Kitly. Under his "practical plan of colonization," 100 English families plus single laborers and mechanics were to be established on 200 square miles of Texas, somewhere on the grant already forfeited by Wavell and Peters.[45]

In April 1849 the company dispatched Dr. Edward Smith to discover potential sites for establishing the proposed colony and to report on its prospects for success based upon the quality of the soil and the region's other resources. Dr. Smith's report to the company was couched solely in superlatives. The soil, he announced, was "universally alluvial" and "in no state have we found finer cattle than in Texas." Texas steers, in fact, "are much superior to ours," being "exceedingly large and always in prime condition." Texas horses, too, "are of a superior quality," and game of all varieties "is in countless numbers over the country." Water, he claimed, was "very excellent and very abundant," markets for all of the farmers' produce were both highly profitable and permanent, and land was to be had "on most easy terms, and required credit is but little."[46]

Under the impetus of such glowing praise, the Universal Emigration and Colonization Company quickly procured 27,000 acres along Cow House Creek, some 100 miles north of Austin, from New York land speculators Richard B. Kimball and James Riley. No sooner were these acres deeded over than the company began enlisting emigrants to settle them. As its chief recruiting agent, the company chose a well-known artist, student of Indian culture and recognized authority on western American life, George Catlin. Between 1829 and 1838 Catlin had painted some 600 portraits of distinguished Indians in their native clothing, as well as many landscapes based upon the scenic beauty of the American West. In 1840 Catlin sailed to Europe, where he spent the next 12 years exhibiting his paintings and lecturing on American Indian lore.[47]

The summer of 1850 found Catlin in the English Midlands, regaling his audiences on the wonders of the Brazos River bottoms. Although at that time Catlin had not yet visited Texas, his thrilling word pictures enthralled thousands of English listeners, and by September the first 117 colonists were poised to sail from Liverpool aboard the Black Star liner, *John Garrou*.[48]

The company planned to send an agent ahead to Cincinnati to purchase wagons, farm implements, draft animals and supplies, and to meet the colonists at New Orleans to lead them to Cow House Creek. At the same time another agent was to have overseen the construction not merely of housing for the immigrants, but a full-scale city! "As many of the families going out are persons of means, education, and perhaps I may add, delicate habits," an officer of the emigration company reported to the *Texas State Gazette*, "we do not like to expose them too much to the ills of a new climate, and so will make what provision we can before hand."[49]

Catlin himself was to have led the pilgrims to their new Eden, but at the last moment abdicated in favor of Sir Edward Belcher, a Captain of the Royal Navy, and Lieutenant Charles Finch Mackenzie of the 41st Welsh Regiment. Almost from the beginning other plans of the colony miscarried as well. The *John Garrou* landed in the fall of 1850 at Galveston rather than at New Orleans, leaving the settlers without transportation at the approach of winter. The 30 English families began their weary trek up the Brazos sustained only by the promise of "a comfortable home [in] a country free from state church, heavy taxation and aristocratic rule." The promise of a brighter future was but dim compensation in the face of the heavy rains, bitter cold, road-less and bridgeless rivers that the colonists faced, and many were disheartened from the start. Among the first to leave the colony and return to England was the company's officer in Texas, Sir Edward Belcher.[50]

Arriving at last at what the company was pleased to call the "City of Kent" in the district of "New Britain," the colonists discovered

"Solomon's Nose," site of the City of Kent, near Kopperl, Bosque County

only an outline of the settlement which they had been led to expect. All lots, cross streets and squares were measured accurately and marked with cedar stakes. The town track proper embraced about 40 acres, and more land was divided into excellent small farms both up and down the Brazos. There was not, however, a single building erected, and for building material, "not even a riding switch" was to be found on the whole 27,000 acres, one colonist reported. Very quickly the colonists of "delicate habits" were pitching tents, excavating dugouts and weaving houses of wattled willow to see them through the miserably harsh central Texas winter.[51]

The country around the "City of Kent" was well suited to cotton, grain and livestock raising, and the colonists planned, as well, to establish "manufactures on an extensive scale." Lieutenant Mackenzie's well-meaning but naive military discipline, the colonists' cultivated and often leisurely habits, crop failure in 1851, vicious Comanche raids and an overabundance of liquor conspired, however, to destroy the colony utterly before the end of its first 12 months.

The son of one of the citizens of Kent recalls how the venture was lost because of Mackenzie's mismanagement. The colonists planted

100 acres in corn that first season and made an excellent crop. "But alas, to show how the English could not meet conditions as they were," just as the corn was in roasting ear, Mackenzie bought a herd of cattle and horses ("on recommendation of their Texas friends who were eager to annex the Englishman's coin") and turned the stock loose on the range. These animals, of course, very quickly invaded the unfenced cornfields and completely destroyed the crop.

Mackenzie owned the colony's only log house and employed the colony's only hired hands. Each morning he would have his men fall in near the house for roll call. They would then march in double file to the fields. Mackenzie, "escorted by his valet, who always carried his gun," would call out " 'Forward,' and just as the enemy [sic] would start to march . . . Mackenzie's . . . wife would call out, 'Captain, that hen refuses to set.' Then he'd holler, 'Halt.' The men would halt and wait until this momentous subject was settled, when once more he would order them to march." These interruptions generally occurred three times per morning, consuming scores of man-hours per week. "Just such army and navy tactics," the citizens of Kent complained, "prevailed in everything the colonists undertook to do."[52]

Hunger, unsanitary conditions and hostile Indians took a terrible toll that year, and before the end of 1851 the "City of Kent" was again as desolate as it had been before the coming of the English. Some moved back to better-established areas of the state, and others returned to England. Some few stuck it out on the frontier and ultimately became successful in the Texas cattle boom of the 1870's. But more of the 117 Englishmen who came to Cow House Creek are there yet, buried near the present city of Waco, victims of a frontier that they were in no way prepared to face.[53]

Texas continued to have an almost hypnotic power over the English imagination, with both land speculators and potential settlers nearly mad for Texas information and for Texan lands. In most cases these men and women came as independent, self-sufficient individuals or as single family members rather than as part of an organized effort at colonization.

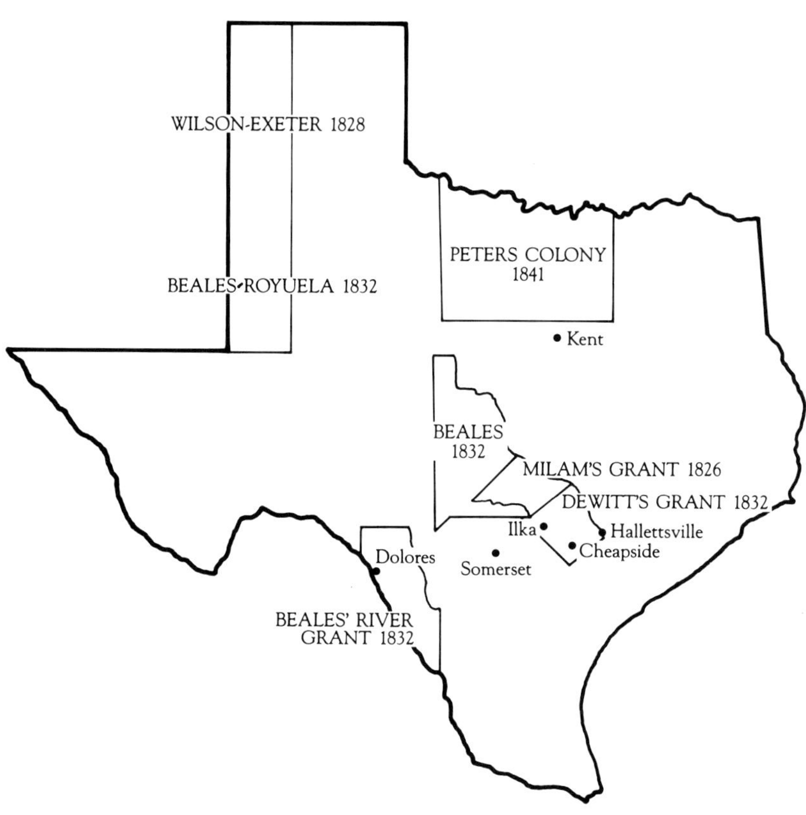

WILSON-EXETER 1828
BEALES-ROYUELA 1832
PETERS COLONY
1841
• Kent
BEALES
1832
MILAM'S GRANT 1826
DEWITT'S GRANT 1832
Ilka •
• Hallettsville
• Cheapside
Dolores
Somerset
BEALES' RIVER
GRANT 1832

The Chroniclers:

A Portfolio of English Writers on the Republic of Texas

C uriosity, a love of adventure, a sense of duty or simple greed drew a host of English men and women to the Republic of Texas. A remarkable number of these visitors kept journals or diaries, wrote reports for their government or company, or published tomes on the nature of the country and its citizens. The degree of partisanship, both pro- and anti-Texan, runs to both extremes, and the magnitude of exaggeration concerning the land's fertility or barrenness, the air's purity or putridity, and the people's honor or knavishness is, at this date, staggering.

As William Kennedy warned "persons who meditate the important act of removal to a new and distant settlement," Texas was not without its "interested eulogists, skillful in softening defects, or throwing them into the background."[1] Likewise the Republic had many detractors, who for a variety of reasons sought with their pens to see the British-American enterprise fail and Mexican sovereignty reinstated.

The reader seeking to know more about Texas, therefore, ought "not merely to peruse the various publications intended for the information of emigrants, but [to] endeavor to ascertain the object of their authors in submitting them to the world."[2] This advice, timely 150 years ago, is no less valid today.

Charles Hooten

A novelist and essayist of small reputation, Charles Hooten sailed with 30 companions from London in December 1840 and arrived in Galveston the following March. Of the 30 travelers in his party, Hooten reported, at least 27 hoped to obtain land and spend "the remainder of their lives [as] good citizens of the new Republic." Not one, said Hooten, was able to accomplish this goal, although many died in the attempt. "May I never again see such ruin of body and fortune, such wreck of heart, as it was my fate to witness in Texas!"[3]

Hooten attributed this failure in part to the ease with which Texas land might be obtained. The English settler, "to whom the idea of possessing landed property is quite new," Hooten observed, was most likely to exhaust all of his capital in buying vast acreage. Fancying himself "equal with some old feudal baron, or the peer of an English Lord," the new Texas freeholder was in fact without the means to cultivate or even to defend his estate.[4]

To Hooten, the land, the elements and the inhabitants of Texas were leagued in diabolical conspiracy to destroy the English immigrant. The heat, the "brick-burned-earth," and the "pestilent, sweltering bayous, in which the fish that cannot escape get cooked (though not literally boiled) to death" contributed to "the complete and total unfitness of this wretched country as a location for English emigrants."[5]

"Broken in health, spirit, and means," Hooten returned to England in November 1842, there to write *St. Louis Isle, or Texiana,* through which he hoped to persuade his countrymen "through the influence of facts," that "for an Englishman to emigrate to Texas . . . is to commit an act of 'temporary insanity.' "

Critics of Hooten's book, both Texans and other readers, have long doubted its author's sanity. One recent commentator in an objective, scholarly critique, characterized Hooten as "able, but debauched and half-crazed." Once in Texas where, this scholar speculates, he was "no longer restrained by the stable English society," he degenerated "into a crude, dissolute, if not savage man." Whatever his motivations or mental condition, the unfortunate

Hooten failed to recover from his Texas experience and died of an overdose of morphine at his Nottingham residence in 1847.[6]

Captain Fredrick Marryat, R.N.

If Charles Hooten had maligned Texas in the British press, he at least did so after spending the better part of a year in the republic and suffering there significant personal and financial losses. Fredrick Marryat, on the other hand, set out to vilify Texas, having neither set foot on its soil nor, so far as is known, having ever met a single Texan.

Already a well-known novelist and a successful naval officer, Marryat set out in 1837 on a tour of the United States and Canada to gather material for a series of travel books which he intended to author. The fruit of his travels was *The Narrative of the Travels and Adventures of Monsieur Violet in California, Sonora, and Western Texas.* Although he never set foot in Texas, he boldly characterized the Texans as "miscreants, cowards, murderers, unjust and delinquent people." Without exception they were "inhospitable, tipplers and brawlers."[7]

NARRATIVE

OF THE

TRAVELS AND ADVENTURES

OF

MONSIEUR VIOLET,

IN

CALIFORNIA, SONORA, & WESTERN TEXAS.

WRITTEN BY

CAPT. MARRYAT, C.B.

IN THREE VOLUMES.

VOL. I.

LONDON:
LONGMAN, BROWN, GREEN, & LONGMANS,
PATERNOSTER ROW.

1843.

Not only was Marryat's venom directed toward the Texan character but toward their cause, freedom from Mexico, as well. Texas's secessionist movement, he announced, was motivated by reports of Texas's great wealth of "gold mines, diamonds, &c." to the greedy speculators of the United States. "If ever there was proof, from the results of pursuing an opposite course, that honesty is the best policy," he told his English readers, "it is to be found in the present state of Texas."[8]

Significantly, the motive behind Marryat's vindictive attack on Texas was an attempt to forestall British recognition of the fledgling republic and the hope that she would be reconquered by Mexico and thus lost to the westward-looking United States. A rock-ribbed English Tory, Marryat made no effort to conceal his prejudices or his intentions. "My object," he boldly stated, "was to do injury to democracy."[9]

Nicholas Doran P. Maillard

During a six-month sojourn in 1840 Nicholas Doran P. Maillard made a slight but favorable impression on the people of Richmond, Texas. Claiming to be an English lawyer, the stranger talked to everyone, took copious notes, wrote what on that culture-starved frontier passed for poetry, and, more important, mixed an excellent drink. For a time he even edited the Richmond *Telescope*. Then, pleading the death of a relative, he returned to England.[10]

Two years later there was published in London a book entitled *The History of the Republic of Texas, From the Discovery of the Country to the Present Time and the Cause of Her Separation From the Republic of Mexico* by N. Doran Maillard, Esq., Barrister-at-Law, of Texas.

According to one student of Texas history, "Of all the snide, scurrilous and cutting attacks ever made against the fair name of the Lone Star Republic (and there have been several) his was the topper."[11] Like Marryat, Maillard sought to discredit Texas in the eyes of the civilized world in hopes of precluding English recognition. Unlike Marryat, however, who acted from genuine if misguided political conviction, Maillard almost surely was acting on instruction from English bankers threatened with the loss of £10,000,000 if Mexico should default on loans secured by Texas land. His justification for his diatribe against Texas, of course, was never admitted to be purely monetary gain. Rather, he represented himself as one "led away by the exaggerated accounts . . . promulgated respecting Texas and the Texans," and seeking only "to prevent more of my own countrymen from sharing in the ruin and wretchedness of too many others who have already emigrated to Texas, and at this moment are either pining there, in want and sickness, or have begged their way out of it. . . ."[12] Misrepresenting the issues and events of the Texas Revolution as greedy treason and Texans as "habitual liars, drunkards, blasphemers, and slanderers, sanguinary gamesters and cold-blooded assassins,"[13] however, Maillard earned his fee.

Francis C. Sheridan

Where there is smoke, there is most often fire. The Englishman with a mind to emigrate to or invest in the Republic of Texas, therefore, might have been well advised to look for other locations for his capital or his home except for the writings of a half-dozen or more fellow Englishmen who saw Texas in a kinder light. Many were the English land speculators who, although coming no closer to Texas than had Captain Marryat, painted its praises in hues more bright than its detractors' were dark. These men were boosting Texas in the English press for reasons as crassly commercial as was N.D.P. Maillard. More objective visitors, however, after careful and unprejudiced examination of Texas, her climate, soils and peoples, pronounced the republic a haven for surplus British pounds and population.

Surely the wittiest and perhaps the best-balanced judgment of Texas during the 1840's was recorded in the private journal of Francis C. Sheridan, an Irishman in the British diplomatic service and grandson of the noted Irish playwright, Richard B. Sheridan. As colonial secretary to the Governor of the Windward Islands, Sheridan was sent to Texas by the Palmerston ministry in order "to contribute the opinion of an eyewitness" to the debate as to whether or not to recognize the republic.[14]

Sheridan's stay in Texas, primarily in Galveston, lasted through the early months of 1840, at the end of which time he recommended recognition to Lord Palmerston. His recommendation was not, however, without reservation. He did not believe, he confided to his journal, that "such a quantity of rogues populates or ever did populate any corner of the globe" as could be found in Texas.[15]

Any fellow countryman intending a visit or move to Texas he advised "to believe as little of the accounts given it, as his credulity will permit of." Although he admitted a great deal of truth in the land speculators' presentation of Texas in the English press, he declared there to be "a great deal more falsehood." So great was Texas's need for settlers and so intense the speculators' quest for profits that from their descriptions of the land "one would suppose Texas was a perfect paradise."[16]

William Kennedy

Among Texas's staunchest partisans of all her English visitors was William Kennedy, Her Majesty's Consul in Galveston from 1842 through 1847. Kennedy first visited Texas in 1838 at the behest of the English government to examine the region's potential for colonization. "After examining the character of the soil, and inquiring into the general resources of the country," Kennedy directed his attention to the "government, religion, laws, police, and manners." He reported in what Maillard calls "Mr. Kennedy's two well puffed up volumes,"[17] "a stable government, religion respected, laws well administered, protection afforded to property and person, and the general tone of manners the same as in the United States."[18]

This glowing account brought a wave of English immigrants to Texas, seeking land for the establishment of cattle and sheep ranches. Those who followed Kennedy's advice to central Texas "were men of wealth and culture, genial and enterprising, who did much toward the development of the county."[19]

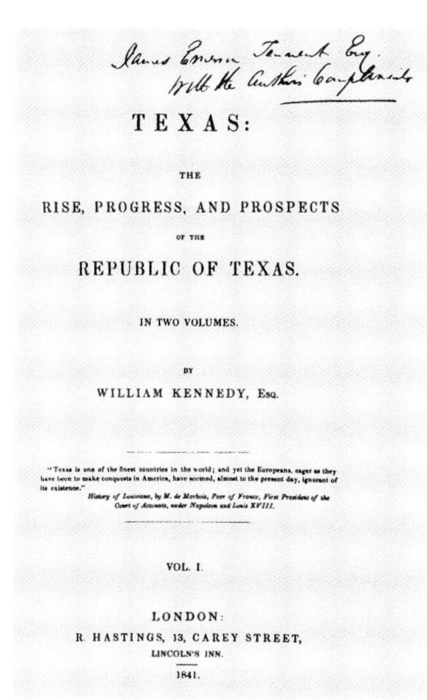

Like those of writers less complimentary toward Texas and her people, William Kennedy's motives for venturing his opinions in print are perhaps somewhat suspect. Kennedy had invested heavily in Texas real estate and in 1842 attempted to interest 600 English families in settling on his Texan holdings. Although the project failed, one might reasonably suspect that much of the praise which Kennedy lavished on Texas and her prospects was in fact nothing more than the customary hyperbole practiced by the salesmen of real estate.

William Bollaert

William Bollaert first came to Texas in 1840 to examine the country and report to the British government but soon came to love the place. A writer, chemist, soldier, geographer, ethnologist and antiquarian, Bollaert was ideally suited to report on Texas's coastline, Indian tribes, botany and natural history, and his native curiosity had given him "a strange inkling to see the new republic."[20]

Bollaert filed his report with the Admiralty and returned to Texas in 1842 "to assist in the survey and examination" of a 4½ million-acre tract to the west of San Antonio "with a view to colonize it with emigrants from Europe."[21] The second Mexican invasion of Texas prevented Bollaert from immediately undertaking his tour of inspection, so, a firm supporter of Texan independence, he enlisted in the Texas Navy and served as sailor aboard the sloop *Lafitte.* "The recollection of having smelt a little powder in the

"Texan Squadron" by William Bollaert

Old World prompted me to lend a willing, although feeble, hand in the New," he later recalled. Following Texas's second war with Mexico, Bollaert took up his deferred exploration of the area surrounding Columbus, Bastrop, Austin and San Antonio, and his job of advising English immigrants on the advantages of settlement there.[22]

By 1844 the imminence of Texas's annexation to the United States quelled the impulse for much British investment in the republic, and Bollaert's failing health caused him to alter his plan for permanent residence in Texas and return to England. He always maintained the greatest respect for the "handful of American farmers, who in an incredibly short period erected their conquest into an independent Republic."[23]

Matilda Charlotte Houstoun

Among Texas's most acute English observers were a pair of ladies: Matilda Charlotte Houstoun, world traveler and author of numerous travel books, and the Honorable Amelia Matilda Murray, maid of honor to Queen Victoria. Mrs. Houstoun, who visited the republic in 1842, believed that "no country has been more calumniated and misrepresented than Texas."[24] Although taken somewhat aback by the "free and easy" manner of American democracy, Mrs. Houstoun was favorably impressed by the hospitality, generosity and good will of the Texans. In *Texas and the Gulf of Mexico* she recounted the tale of an Englishman who, "not possessed of much ready cash," found that "a good song, or a budget of news, invented or remembered," would always be taken in payment for a night's lodging and an ample meal.[25]

She severely castigated the Texans who were "too indolent either to plant vegetables, shoot game, or catch fish," but found them willing to undertake any project except those which demand "steady and settled habits of industry."[26] In fact, she opined, "where an Englishman would sink, past redemption, in the mire of despondency," the Texans, "to their praise and credit be it spoken, continue to struggle through."[27]

Owning neither Texas lands nor Mexican bonds, Mrs. Houstoun probably viewed the Lone Star Republic with a considerably less prejudiced eye than many of her male fellow visitors, and her commentary is, therefore, probably among the most accurate and reliable.

Amelia Matilda Murray

"You will think me adventurous to undertake this," wrote Amelia Matilda Murray to an English friend in 1855, "but these new countries are so interesting to a person fond of Natural History and fine scenery, that one makes up one's mind to undergo some inconvenience and difficulty." At age 66, therefore, this lady-in-waiting to Queen Victoria landed at Galveston for a whirlwind tour through Houston, Washington-on-the-Brazos, Huntsville and Nacogdoches, and then down the Red River to New Orleans.

She found Texas a beautiful country, resembling "Somersetshire, Kent, and Winsor [sic] Forest by turns" and reported that she "should much prefer settling in Texas to any other part of the Union . . . unless it was the highlands of Virginia."[28]

Of the people, she was less fond. Like Mrs. Houstoun she was somewhat offended by the easy familiarity of frontier democracy, finding "the servant class" almost too impudent to be tolerated. To the Negroes she found it "necessary to scold or speak sharply before they will bestir themselves," and white servants she found to be proud and easily offended by what she, as an English aristocrat, thought the simplest and most logical demands.

Unlike the English gentlemen who traveled the frontier, accepting Texas's crude but generous hospitality as they found it, Lady Amelia abominated the state's hotels, finding them "careless and troublesome beyond measure."[29]

Prejudiced only by the beliefs and habits of her class and not by hope of financial gain, Lady Amelia's account of Texas as she saw it is factual if highly opinionated. Although generally favorable in her treatment of the Texans, her aristocratic background made her severely critical of institutions dear to the democratic American tradition.

Amelia Edith Huddleston Barr

Among the English women in Texas Charles Hooten noted "many a longing eye, that too often gazes afar upon the vision of its birthplace." Only very few, he wrote, "are the emigrant females of Texas who would not gladly go back again to the respective places from which they came."[30] One English woman who would surely qualify as an exception to Hooten's generalization is Amelia Barr, the daughter of a Lancashire Presbyterian minister who spent the happiest years of her life in Texas.

Mrs. Barr, with her husband, Robert, and their two daughters, arrived at the mouth of Buffalo Bayou in 1856 and from there traveled overland to Austin where Mr. Barr became secretary to the legislative Ways and Means Committee. On their trek into the interior Mrs. Barr "was transported" by the beauty of the Texas scenery. The prairies and hills, the flowers and wildlife "went to the heart like wine," she rhapsodized, but best of all were the people. On the steamer trip up the bayou toward Harrisburg, the Barrs passed the site of San Jacinto, where "Houston and his eight hundred gentlemen, wiped out the Spanish army under Santa Anna, and gave American settlers in Texas that religious and civic liberty which was their right."[31]

The boat's captain, she wrote, bared his head as they sailed by the battlefield and related "the gallant, stirring story" of the Texas Revolution which she later fictionalized in *Remember the Alamo*, one of her 70 published novels.

Deeply impressed by the example of "men who had at least once in their lives scorned the mean god Mammon," and risked their lives for "their God and their country," Mrs. Barr commented, "We are going to live among heroes. . . . After a life among weavers and traders, will not that be a great experience?"[32]

The Barr family spent five idyllic years in Austin prior to 1861 and during the Civil War behaved with all of the heroism of their bravest Texan neighbors. With the fall of the Confederacy and the region's attendant economic collapse, they sought to better their fortunes in Galveston, where the awesome yellow fever epidemic of 1867 killed Robert Barr and his two young sons within a 24-hour period.

Texas lost its charm for Amelia Barr, and she and her daughters moved to New York where she began her literary career, one of the most prolific of the 19th century. Nevertheless, as her novel of the Texas Revolution and several chapters of her autobiography *All the Days of My Life* indicate, the beauty, hospitality and bold spirit of the Lone Star State always remained among her fondest memories.

Amelia Barr

Chapter 3
Divided by a Common Language

Although English colonization efforts without exception failed in Texas, individual Englishmen continued to leave their mother country for new homes in the American West. From the end of the Mexican War until the outbreak of the Civil War, depressed economic conditions in England and a boom in international cotton and grain prices induced hundreds of English families to "renounce forever all allegiance and fidelity to any foreign Prince, Potentate, State or Sovereign whatsoever, and particularly any and all allegiance to the Queen of Great Britain and Ireland" and to swear an oath at Galveston or Indianola to "bear true allegiance to the United States and support the Constitution of the same."

Thomas Steele, one such young man who departed from Old England bound for America, wrote to his father, "I wish I could transport you here for one half-hour to see some of my fellow emigrants all full of hope and Spirit." Yet, he continues, but for the "John Bullism" of their spirits, each seems "as unfitted for such an enterprize one would think as their greatest enemy could wish." Rather than seasoned farmers, the force of pioneers that England was sending to America, Steele observed, was composed chiefly of clerks, haberdashers, chemists "and one bookseller from Dover."[1]

Leaving Old England for America

Despite Steele's misgivings, however, one historian of the transatlantic migration, Charlotte Erickson, has opined that "perhaps no other immigrants came so well prepared psychologically as the English." The skilled workers and farmers who settled here were able to retain or raise the income level and social rank that they had enjoyed in England while the smaller group "who found life without servants unacceptable or who were offended by the brashness of American ways usually could afford to return home." Indeed, few apparent obstacles blocked the English immigrant from full assimilation into American culture. Similarity in language, customs, and economic and political organization would seem to have offered the British almost instant acceptance in their new American communities. Especially in the rural society of the Texas frontier, English newcomers were unlikely to feel any pressure from American natives to conform to any local customs or attitudes except those condoning slavery. The English were freely accepted into frontier churches and were welcome to take part in local political activities. "Indeed," says Erickson, "it is difficult to imagine circumstances more propitious to the rapid assimilation of an immigrant group than these British immigrants met in rural America."[2]

Yet for all of the promise of wealth and happiness held out to the English emigrant by the State of Texas, tragedy too often attended the newcomer's attempts to establish himself there. English traveler Charles Hooten was one of a "glad, active, and hopeful band" which came to Texas in 1841. Less than two years later he returned to England to write of the utter failure of his party's hopes and of the absolute falsehood of "glorious Texan promises." Most of his companions had died in Texas. Those who survived, he claimed, were broken in health and resources, and held but one last faint hope: of "once more reaching the home of their birth alive."[3]

The question endlessly debated in both the Texan and the English press was whether Texas itself was culpable for many circumstances such as Hooten described, or whether the unprepared Englishman carried the seeds of his own destruction in his baggage from home. William Bollaert, another English traveler and stout partisan of Texas, presented a counter argument to Hooten's diatribe against the state. "Two Englishmen left their native country," reads Bollaert's parable, "one on his way to Texas, the other to Illinois." On their arrival at New Orleans the Texas-bound traveler listened to tales such as Hooten's, immediately took fright and returned home on the next ship bound for London. The other was fascinated by what he heard of Texas and determined to pay the place a visit. After remaining a few days in

Two Englishmen go into a store at Weimar.

"Aw, 'ave you got henny Lea & Perrin's Wor'ster sauce?"

"No: don't keep it, sir; never heard of it."

"Never 'eard of it! By Jove, what a blawsted country!"

Turning to the other exile,
" 'Arry, let's go back to hold Hengland."

Galveston he moved into the hinterlands. "He was delighted with the country, and has settled in the vicinity of Gonzales, on the Guadalupe River, and when heard of last, he was about to be married to the daughter of a rich old Mexican rancher."[4]

The moral of Bollaert's probably apocryphal tale is obviously that a land such as Texas required a settler of boldness of spirit, determination and industry. These it would generously reward. All others the frontier would reject with whatever degree of harshness the situation demanded. In the era of first and hottest debate over Charles Darwin, Herbert Spencer and the theory of "the survival of the fittest," Texas was a living laboratory, daily demonstrating that the strong should prosper while the lesser individuals would be rightly relegated to history's scrap heap.

Of all English commentators on the chances of their countrymen prospering in Texas, Arthur Ikin was probably most balanced in his appraisal and advice. "The greater number of English emigrants, from their previous habits of life, and their incapability of forming a just idea of the real state of things," he observed, "make at *first* but very indifferent settlers, and but poor judges of the advantages or drawbacks of any particular settlement." The "more hardy and enterprising" Americans and Scots, the "more easily contented" Germans, and those English settlers who had faced the Canadian winter and the Australian drought, however, Ikin assured his readers, would testify that there is no other new country "where the hardships are so light, and the ultimate reward so certain, as the Republic of Texas."[5]

However easy, relative to the experiences of their countrymen on other continents or of non-English-speaking immigrants in America, relocation in Texas for Englishmen might have been, physical and emotional hardships were undeniable. Even those who came to Texas directly from English farms found American agricultural methods different from those to which they were accustomed, and the breaking of virgin land was a task unperformed by the British for centuries.[6]

Although few English immigrants suffered from food shortage, meals were uniformly monotonous since exotic produce was almost totally unavailable on the frontier. No matter to what they had been accustomed in the old country, almost all farmers and their families wore only homespun in Texas. Although the more hardy among these pioneers came to regard anything homemade as morally superior to manufactured items, doubtlessly many farm women longed bitterly for the more comfortable, not to mention fashionable, fabrics they had worn at home.

Housing for the immigrant family was almost invariably of a lower standard in Texas than they had known in England, at least in the early years. Few proper English ladies were prepared for the reality of a log cabin or a dugout. A house without proper floors, plaster, fireplace, windows or furniture was a genuine hardship, and more than one English matron lamented to friends at home of the necessity of "barbarizing in a log hut" until a real house could be constructed.[7]

Another bitter adjustment required of the English immigrant was the acceptance of the lower level of services, both private and public, provided in Texas. "The poorest man in the old country thinks nothing of a road or path, or a drink of water from a well," wrote one disgruntled pioneer who noted that Texas seldom provided these accommodations. Transportation and communication links were invariably poorer in the American West than in England, and the lack of forges, mills, breweries and public houses were also the topic of much complaint.[8]

The want of cultural amenities, too, was severely felt by gently bred English immigrants. As late as 1856, one newcomer recorded, there were but two pianos in all of Austin. No bookstore existed, and books

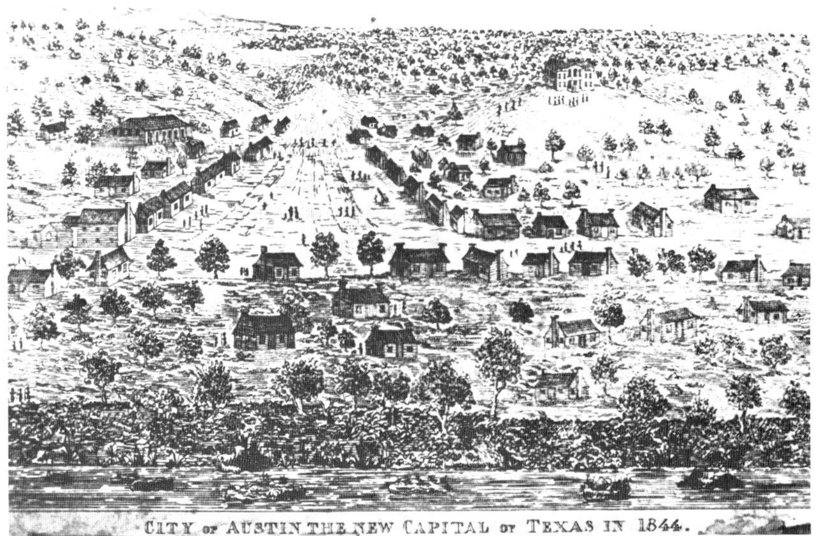

were not evident in private homes. Too few were theaters, concert and lecture halls, and public entertainments of any kind.[9]

Far worse in most cases than physical privation and hardship was the psychological wrench felt by English settlers in remote Texas. Although the British seldom lived apart from native Americans, loneliness was often quite intense and the feeling of isolation profound. As one lonely immigrant phrased it, "The English tongue is practically all that is English in America." Indeed, Erickson speculates, the immigrant who came from a non-English-speaking nation might possess "a built-in shield against painful encounters" with Texas society. "The Englishman in America," she believes, "was more exposed because his difficulties were not so apparent." The English Texan was, however, an easily identifiable aberration from the Anglo-American norm.[10]

Francis Sheridan recorded in his diary that the Texans were "delighted at the visit of . . . Britishers," and "would much sooner see an Englishman in Texas than any one from the U. States."[11] Although the typical representative of the English race was perceived to be honest, energetic and of a practical turn of mind, other traits which he brought from Great Britain were not so well calculated to engender success in taming a vast frontier.

Mrs. Houstoun suggested that "our countrymen in particular . . . should settle in herds, because they generally have a defect in the character which stands in the way of their success as settlers." This "defect," which she did not find among the Americans, was "the difficulty they find in adapting themselves to occupations to which they have been unaccustomed."[12] This characteristic had its positive aspects. Much admired was the English gentleman "who despite the crudeness of his surroundings refused to succumb to environment," and "who despite the questionable character of many of his early associates, refused to be victimized by the looseness and immorality" of his Texan neighbors.[13]

The other side of this coin, however, was the Englishman's incapacity to adapt himself to new conditions or ideas. One vivid but none too serious example of the unwillingness of English gentlemen to adapt to the ways of the frontier was recorded by Amelia Barr. Of considerable amusement to her were the dissimilarities in her husband's style of dress and that of his friend, a member of the state legislature: Mr. Barr's high silk hat "typified the quality and fashion of all the garments beneath it," she recalls, and she was certain that he was the only man in Austin in 1857 wearing gloves. His Texan companion by way of "picturesque contrast" was dressed in a white flannel shirt, dark tweed trousers and a broad leather belt *without furnishings.* Whether in defiance or ignorance of prevailing gentleman's fashion, the Texan legislator wore "very low cut shoes" rather than the obligatory Wellingtons, and Mrs. Barr "hardly [thought] his hands had ever dreamed of gloves." On his head the Texan wore "a handsome black sombrero, with a silver cord and tassel round it."

The lady admitted that she was "forcibly impressed" with the fitness of Texan garb for the Texas climate, but stated that her proper British husband was "wedded to his waistcoat, ashamed to go to the street without a proper coat, and quite sure he would not feel respectable without his suspenders."[14] In the words of one Texan, "An Englishman, as a rule, is a pig-headed, self-conceited animal, who religiously believes himself better than all creation." Although he conceded that once through the "process of adaption" the English settler could be as good as the best Texan, he also maintained that he "is no use as a workman till he has been here three years, and got the pride and stupidity knocked out of him."[15]

Captain Charles Elliot agreed, finding his countrymen over-refined for success on the frontier. "English people are broken in, or should I say broken *down* to do but one thing in the world," he wrote. This want of flexibility led Elliot to observe that "in this country they made but sorry work of it in taming the wilds, compared with the

Houston, 1856

American races." Elliot's experience had taught him that the English system of military, social and political training rendered men unfit for "roughness and reverses." The English "must all work together perfectly or it will hardly work at all." The Texans, on the other hand, *"jolt* and *jar* terrifically in their progress, but *on* they do get, and prosper too, under circumstances when our people would starve to death."[16]

Mrs. Houstoun, too, was favorably impressed by the vigor and determination of the native Texan. On a visit to the new republic in 1842 she noted that "not a day passes without being marked by some endeavor (often a successful one) of these energetic settlers to raise their country into strength and prosperity." The much-remarked American zeal, however, was one of the few Texan traits which the British accepted as unalloyed virtue.[17]

Texanophile Charles Elliot found the natives to be "rough and wild," but much admired their courage and consistency. Captain Elliot, in fact, could "hardly know any more fearful and humiliating subject of reflection" than the helplessness of the English settler against "these scheming, enterprising, and . . . better informed" Texans.[18] Another military man, Lieutenant Colonel Arthur J.L. Fremantle of Her Majesty's Coldstream Guards, years later agreed that "in spite of their peculiar habits of hanging, shooting, and *c.* . . . there was much to like" about the Texans. During his travels in the Confederate States in 1863, Fremantle found Texans to possess "a sort of bon-hommie honesty and straightforwardness, a natural courtesy and extreme good nature, which was very agreeable."[19]

N. Doran Maillard, on the other hand, strongly averred that there was "not a subject connected with the history of Texas, that has been so grossly misrepresented, as that of the character . . . of the white population." In his 1842 *History of the Republic of Texas* this English observer declared Texas to be "a country filled with habitual liars, drunkards, blasphemers, and slanderers; sanguinary gamesters and cold-blooded assassins; with idleness and sluggish indolence (two vices for which the Texans are already proverbial); with pride, engendered by ignorance and supported by fraud."[20]

English novelist and world traveler Fredrick Marryat was also of Maillard's opinion. "It is much to be lamented," he wrote in 1843, "that Texas had not been populated by a more deserving class of individuals." Had this been the case, he believes, Texas might early have become one of the powers of the earth, but the region's potential was lost when it became "the resort of every vagabond and scoundrel who could not venture to remain in the United States." This supposed influx of social jetsam fixed the cultural status of the republic, in Marryat's mind, at least, as "wholly destitute of principle or probity," beyond the means of "more respectable settlers" to amend.[21]

Only slightly more complimentary was Francis Sheridan's humorous view of the character of the native Texan. "I would not wish to convey to the reader the idea, that the population of Texas universally speaking are a set of ragamuffins," he confided to his diary while on a visit to Galveston. "On the contrary, there are individual instances of talent, worth & responsibility, & on the exertion & character of these men depend the future prosperity of Texas." On the whole, however, Sheridan did not believe "such a quantity of rogues populates or ever did populate any corner of the globe."[22]

Hardly a single aspect of the Texan character, in fact, escaped the close scrutiny of the English immigrant or tourist, and concerning each of these aspects controversy was sure to exist. As might be surmised from the differences of opinion among Elliot, Fremantle, Maillard, Marryat and Sheridan, the honesty of the average Texan was a source of warm debate.

Anti-Texan Englishmen, such as those cited above, pointed to Texas as the ultimate haven for scoundrels—a haven for the fugitives from justice from half the civilized world. So great was the concentration of outlaws and cutthroats, these image makers insisted, that each Texan greeted the other with the question, "What war yer name afore yer moved to these parts?" and the initials G.T.T. "Gone to Texas"—were known as an internationally used symbol for runaway criminals.

While even Colonel Fremantle agreed that Texas was "the most lawless state in the Confederacy,"[23] other English travelers tended to rank Texans "very high" in honesty. Charles Hooten, for example, normally no friend of Texas or the Texans, commented that "it is at once a remarkable and pleasing fact to record, that petty larcenies of any description are as rare, either in towns or in the prairie, as in [England] they are common."[24]

Instruments of the much-noted Texas mayhem were fascinating to English observers. "Every person we met carried a six-shooter," marveled Colonel Fremantle, "although it is very seldom necessary to use them."[25] Ironically, the ubiquitous Bowie knife, so much remarked by English diarists, letter writers and novelists, was most often manufac-

G. T. T.

tured in Sheffield or Birmingham "and brought over in British Ships as a profitable Speculation."[26]

As to the veracity of the average Texan—whose tendency to exaggerate, boast or out-and-out lie about his state's natural wonders has long been legendary—the English were equally mixed in their reaction. Although many were put off by the tellers of tall tales, others were delighted by them. Edward Smith explained the Texan's tendency to hyperbole, reminding his readers that the limitless resources of the state and the enviable prosperity of its citizens gives the habit of using "exaggerated expressions of feeling, and the positive and comparative are less frequently employed than the superlative."[27]

Other habits of speech were also much discussed by English auditors. The fastidious Hooten remarks the "peculiar characteristic of the state of refinement and social intercourse" of Texans to be "their inveterate habit of swearing and cursing." Awed by "its very excess, its depth and recklessness," he notes that the substance of communication often "flows into and becomes lost in an ocean of oaths, like a fresh stream in a putrid sea—oaths too of a character so entirely new and diabolical, that one would be apt to imagine the genius of Depravity herself had been taxed to her utmost powers to produce them for the especial use of this rising State."[28] Less loquacious but still in complete agreement was Fremantle. The Texan "never opens his mouth without an oath," he recorded, and that "strictly American in its character."[29]

Another of the Texan's social customs which both appalled and fascinated the English was his capacity, or at least taste, for strong drink. After trekking from Brownsville, "the rowdiest town of Texas," to San Antonio, Fremantle wrote that he had become "comparatively accustomed and reconciled to the necessity of shaking hands and drinking brandy with everyone," a necessity, he remarks, which "does not exist except in Texas."[30] Sheridan had noted 20 years earlier that the "passion for erecting grog shops in Texas, supersedes the thirst of religious worship & Temples wherein to exercise it,"[31] and Marryat had observed that when Austin became the capital of the republic, the tiny city's three hotels played host mightily to the president, secretaries, judges, ministers and members of Congress. All, said the English observer, were "more or less tipsy," and in the quarrels that inevitably broke out, "hardly a night passed without four or five men being stabbed or shot."[32]

Edward Smith, as usual taking a more charitable view of the Texans, reported observing but one case of intemperance during his visit to the Lone Star Republic. He does admit, however, to having been told that "an intemperate use of whiskey is far too common in every class of society."[33]

Brownsville, 1865

Far worse to English sensibilities than the habit of excessive drinking, a "depraved taste" which, after all, pervaded "most of the classes" of England, were two other examples of Texan "degeneracy": the "filthy habits" of overindulgence in tobacco and underindulgence in bathing. Although in most instances the stoutest champion of Texan virtues, Smith chides his favorites for their want of familiarity with soap and water. "It is probable that the people of Texas are as cleanly of their persons . . . as those of other States," he reported, "but they are far from cleanly. They have great natural facilities for bathing, but we scarcely found a Texan who took advantage of them."[34]

Smith was perhaps the only 19th century English visitor to Texas who made note of its citizens' distaste for the bath, but almost all commented upon their indulgence in tobacco. Sheridan complained bitterly that all of the Texan's time "is spent talking and chewing." A subject which he thought almost too "nasty" to record nevertheless occupied Sheridan for many paragraphs. "No one who has not seen & suffered by this most disgusting custom," he maintained, "can form the faintest idea how universal & incessant is the practice. Hig[h] & low, rich & poor, young & old, chew, chew, chew & spit, spit, spit all the blessed day & most of the night—& as the spitting-box is considered generally speaking a superfluous luxury the floors of the rooms & fireplaces bear ample testimony to the beastly habits of their occupants."[35] G.W. Featherstonhaugh, in his two-volume *Excursions Through the Slave States*, echoes Sheridan's disgust. Having found Texas's hotels rather worse than primitive, Featherstonhaugh relates his discomfort at having to share accommodations with a native traveler. "Of all of the distressing situations in which I could be placed," he wrote, "the keenest of all would be to be compelled to pass the night on the same bed with another man, and that man a stranger, a tobacco eater, and perpetual expectorator."[36]

Colonel Fremantle was amazed to note that *only five* of his nine fellow passengers on a Texas stagecoach chewed tobacco during the night, and these "aimed at the window with great accuracy, and didn't *splash* me." A bit unnerved by the continual crossfire of tobacco juice, however, Fremantle confesses that the amount of sleep he got that night "was naturally very trifling." With the dawn "tobacco chewing became universal," and the chewers' accuracy "was sometimes a little wild." This proper Victorian gentleman was no little daunted by the "shower of tobacco juice from the mouths of the Southern chivalry on the roof."[37]

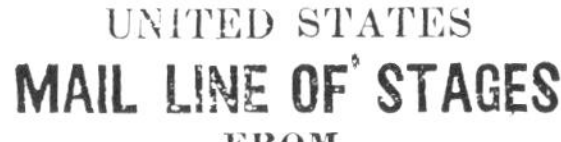

The subscribers, contractors to carry a week-ly mail from Port Lavaca to New Braunfels, via Victoria, Cuero, Gonzales, and Seguin, purposes running a line of four horse stages on the above route.

Leaves Port Lavaca on Friday's, at 6 a. m., and arrives at New Braunfels on Mondays' at 4 o'clock, p. m.

Returning, leaves New Braunfels on Saturday's, at 6 a. m., and arrives at Port Lavaca on Tuesday's at 4 p. m.

RATES.

Port Lavaca, M. H. Nicholson, agent.
F'm Lavaca to Victoria, $2 50—G. W. Wright
" Victoria to Cuero, 2 50—I R. North.
" Cuero to Gonzales, 2 50—C. S. Brown.
" Gonzales to Seguin, 2 50—J. S. Galvert.
" Seguin to Braunfels, 2 50—S. Millett
" New Braunfels to San
    Antonio, 2 50—

Every care and attention will be paid to the comfort and convenience of passengers.

HARRISON & BROWN,
Proprietors.

Victoria, Oct. 26th, 1849.

SALTMARSH'S
LINE OF UNITED STATES MAIL STAGES
D. A. SALTMARSH & Co., *Proprietors.*
From Indianola to San Antonio, via Lavaca, Victoria, Yorktown, Sulphur Springs and Eclato.

THE subscriber takes pleasure in announcing that he has on this Line good Troy coaches, with good teams, and polite drivers—leaving Indianola on the arrival of the steamers from New Orleans, for San Antonio and touching at the above points. The country through which this route passes is one of much beauty and interest to the traveler, (including the Sulphur Springs,) and the roads are good.

For further particulars apply at the stage office, Alhambra Hotel, Indianola.

J. R. FRETWELL, Agent.
Indianola, Feb. 1852. [1:tf.

Advertisement from The Indianola Bulletin

Advertisement from The Texian Advocate, *Victoria,* January 11, 1850

Among Fremantle's fellow travelers was General Sam Houston, whom the Englishman quickly sized up as "a remarkable and clever man," but one "much given to chewing tobacco, and blowing his nose with his fingers."[38]

If Fremantle was nonplussed by the chewing and spitting habits of "the Southern chivalry," William Bollaert was utterly aghast at the many Texas "ladies" who dipped snuff ("which means putting it in their mouths instead of their noses"). This English worthy, however, maintained his sense of gallantry and noted that those women he had questioned on the practice "had the grace to confess it was not a delicate accomplishment."[39] N. Doran Maillard, a perpetual Texanaphobe, described the women of Texas with far less gallantry, referring only to their alleged want of style, grace and charm. Texas women, he reported, "have little neatness or cleanliness of person to attract the eye." He further libeled Texas womanhood with the outrageous opinion that "their figures are scarcely to be described; coarse from neglect, or emaciated by self-indulgence; their skins have borrowed from the sun," he claims, "the exact hue of the lemon; and if countenance be a true index of the mind, their dispositions are also like the lemon."[40]

William Bollaert, however, came to the defense of the fairer sex, expressing the view that such a cad as Maillard had not been admitted to the society of ladies in Texas and had consorted only with the crudest level of society.[41] Sheridan, always the clever cynic, described Texas's women as "very pretty and all well-dressed, vulgar and awkward," much as one might suspect in a prosperous frontier society.[42] Kindest to the women of Texas were the ladies who visited from England. Mrs. Houstoun, for example, commented that "the fair 'ladies of the land' are as delicate and refined in their habits, as they are well educated and beautiful."[43] Mrs. Amelia Barr also noted a class of Texas women who "chewed snuff without cessation," but mitigated the vice with the observation that the majority of women who "dipped" had likely formed the habit "when it was their only physical tranquilizer through days and nights of terror, and pain, and watchfulness." The habit, once formed, she allowed, was not easily broken.[44] Mrs. Houstoun also observed with no little satisfaction that Texas women "have unbounded influence over and are treated with marked respect and consideration" by their suitors and husbands. This latter is scarcely surprising in an area where men outnumbered women by a ratio of five to three.[45]

The Anglo-American settlers on the Texas frontier, overwhelmingly of Southern origin and now living far from neighbors or centers of communication, were starved for news and conversation. These two factors combined to make Texan hospitality another item on which English travelers were in universal agreement. Fremantle, for example, noted that "a person incapable of protecting himself is always sure of kind treatment and compassion, even from the wildest Texans."[46] Mrs. Houstoun, too, had "reason to speak gratefully of the courtesy and civility of the Texans," and believed that their spirit of helpfulness and goodwill was a natural result of their frontier condition. Texas, she believed, was then in that phase of development "before refinement begets selfishness, and the indulgence of luxuries hardens the heart."[47]

Bollaert also had the "good fate" of meeting and being offered the hospitality of great planters as well as small farmers. In the establishments of both classes he "uniformly received every kindness." The hotels and inns of Texas, however, he and all of his English fellow travelers found wanting. The highly adventurous Bollaert, who in his younger years had been among the first Europeans to cross the fierce

Atacama Desert of Chile, pronounced Texas hotels "not quite so récherché as Fenton's or Long's," but stated that he had been "perfectly contented" in them. In this he was unique among his peers.[48] Maillard found them to be "conducted in the most miserable way, being extremely filthy, filled with vermin of every description, and wretchedly supplied with food," all at exorbitant prices. In this opinion Maillard was with the vast majority.[49]

Sheridan found the "regulations attending to the feeding" at Galveston's Tremont House to be "strictly American." The doors to the dining room were thrown open, and the boarders "rush head-long in, & in less than ten minutes rush head-long out again."[50]

Tremont House.

GALVESTON,

THE Undersigned having leased this well known Hotel, has had the same thoroughly renovated and refurnished and is now prepared to accommodate the travrl ing public.

Nov. 17 ly.   R. H. MONTGOMERY.
Lessee.

TREMONT HOUSE.

GALVESTON, TEYAS.

Price of Board:

Board and Lodging per day,	$2 00
Children and servants,	50
Breakfast,	50
Dinner,	75
Supper,	50
Lo ging,	75
Day Boarders per month,	25 00

Permanent Board and Lodging according to the room occupied.   R, R. MONTGOMERY.

Jan 16 3m.

Advertisement from The Weekly Telegraph, *Houston, April 1, 1857*

English commentators found Texas cuisine to be exotic at best and unpalatable too often. Edward Smith reported that although the Texan "lives in a very Goshen," almost every article is "fried over the fire; so that the surfeiting fried chicken, and the everlasting hog and hominy" become endlessly monotonous.[51] Not so monotonous but equally barbarous were the meals served to Mrs. Houstoun. Texas suppers, she recorded, "consisted of alternate dishes of boiled oysters, and beef steaks" of which both were in plenty, and the steaks especially "disappeared in marvellously quick time between the strong jaws of the Texan gentlemen." As for the quality of the beef, the English lady confessed to preferring "meat which has been kept somewhat more than an hour," and related an instance while cruising the Texas coast when dinner was delayed for some time, while the cook went on shore and

"shot a beef."[52] Mrs. Barr, who spent 11 years in Texas, found meals served in Austin and other urban areas to be quite satisfactory but was appalled by "the continuous meal of bacon" served in east Texas rural areas. "Throughout our journey there had been myriads of cattle around us," she recorded, "but nothing except bacon to eat—hundreds of thousands of milk cows, but rarely, indeed, either milk, butter, or cheese on the table."[53]

Advertisements from The Weekly Telegraph, *Houston, December 28, 1859*

To the educated English palate the Texas libations were if anything worse than the viands, and the table manners worst of all. Sheridan recalls "a wine they called Sherry" which tasted "something like Chilli vinegar & Bilge water," and comments on the Texas practice of feeding oneself "chiefly with the knife."[54] In sum, Hooten reflects, "when a Texan multitude is to be fed, why, fed they must be, if there be anything within reach to lay hands on."[55]

If the English who came to Texas in the early 19th century were awed by Texas drinking, disgusted by Texas spitting and chewing, charmed by Texas hospitality and dyspeptic from Texas cooking, they were utterly baffled by Texas politics. Although political freedom was always a principal drawing card which America offered to its immigrants, democracy, frontier-style, was often as repellent to the class-conscious and orderly English as was a woman dipping snuff. True, the English generally wished to escape the authority of over-powering government and its crushing taxes. Yet when the average immigrant spoke of "freedom," it was specifically freedom from taxation to which he referred. The Queen's former subjects cared little for participation in the democratic process.[56]

Although many English-born Texans held local offices, as a whole they lagged behind other immigrants in seeking U.S. citizenship and often expressed a positive distaste for the rough-and-tumble of American political life. This disinclination to enter into public affairs in their new country was largely a result of the English class system wherein hereditary rank ordering precluded a change in social status by election. Those who were from the more comfortable classes, those who had been accustomed to keeping servants and who were not greatly influenced by the Baptist or Methodist emphasis on humility, came to Texas already convinced of their own superiority to the natives whom they most often saw as ignorant and crude. These new Texans resisted meeting their neighbors on terms of social or political equality and avoided assimilation into the democratic process.[57] Colonel Fremantle, for example, was amused at the Texan notion that since "every white man is as good as another (by theory), and every white female is by courtesy a lady, there is only one class."[58] Robert Williams concurred, observing that "every white man, however poor, if he were honest and decently behaved, was *socially* the equal of those in power and authority; and to gain power and position it was not necessary to be wealthy, only to be popular; in fact, to be a *man*."[59] Mrs. Barr agreed that "*colour* not money was the dividing line," in consequence of which "every good white man was the social equal of every other good white man." Somewhat more astute than Fremantle or Williams, however, she added that "women are never democrats. There is always in their societies an exclusive set."[60]

In democratic theory the only rank is official rank, and all others are equal. G.W. Featherstonhaugh saw this theoretical equality as far other than "*practical* equality, which seems to be beyond the powers of demonstration." Although the laws of a country "may require all men to be equally stupid" or to "forbid any man to have a more lofty nature than the rest, and may declare that the top and the bottom are one and the same thing," the mere legislation would not make it so. All of these principles, declared Featherstonhaugh, "may be proclaimed on the 4th of July from Dan to Beersheba," but competition with its relative successes and failures will yet go on. In America of all places, he observed, the rivalry for "the almighty dollar" was intense, and "a superabundance" of wealth had become "a substitute for other virtues" and "stands in the place of all distinction."[61]

Less scathing in her attack on the theory of American democracy but equally repelled by its product was Mrs. Houstoun. When the keeper of an inn at which she was lodging joined her party at dinner and began to take part in the conversation, she was at first quite scandalized at his "free and easy" manner. "How surprised we should be in England at such familiarity," she wrote. In Texas, however, one soon senses the impropriety of taking offence. The transgressors, she perceived, "are so very far from intending incivility," but are rather "so genuinely kind" that she "felt inclined to take everything as it was meant—in good part."[62]

If socializing with the citizens of the Texas frontier was distasteful to the English gentry, engaging in the democratic process was amusing at best and disgusting at worst. "Canvassing for election is not one of the least amusing operations carried on occasionally amongst the various dispersed communities of Texas," Hooten informed his readers. Barroom debates, "enlivened now and then by the glitter of a bowie-knife and a stream of blood amongst the crowd," dance parties "to which ladies not exactly as virtuous as nuns have access," and barbeques are all part of the train with which every candidate lays siege to public office. The highest conviction which Hooten observed in any office seeker was that "without plenty to eat, drink, and smoke, no good whatever under heaven" could come of his candidacy.

On election day Hooten gravitated back and forth between Galveston's two taverns, each of which was the stronghold of a rival faction. "Brandy and ice-water were the order of every moment," with the bars crowded to capacity and the names of the candidates "literally shrieked and yelled by half-frantic voters in each other's ears throughout the town."[63]

Galveston, 1844

The lower orders of English society, of course, were much less prejudiced against American democratic institutions and often rose within the system that their "betters" were resisting and belittling. More important than political contact with their new neighbors were the social contacts the English immigrants made with Texans through the churches. Religion was one of the strongest ties common to both the English and the native-born farmer. Although the upper classes were staunchly Anglican in their faith, the majority of the lower orders came from a variety of Protestant denominations including Presbyterian, Methodist and Baptist. From his religious beliefs the immigrant found help in sustaining reverses and living far from family and friends, and in the congregation he found a point of contact with the more settled elements of the Texan community.[64]

From beginnings such as these the English immigrant was assimilated into Texas society. Despite the hardships that sent some immigrants back to England and despite the crudeness of their new surroundings when compared with their homeland, most Englishmen who came to Texas in the first half of the 19th century stayed, prospered and were soon indiscernible from their American-born neighbors. Second-generation English Texans often, in fact, spoke with pure Texas accents as contrasted with the clipped intonations of their parents. Lillie Barr Munroe, daughter of an English mother and a Scottish father, remembers the surprise of first hearing her parents speaking of Great Britain as home. Although herself born in England, so accustomed was she to her Austin home that she was a schoolgirl before she realized "that we were not Texas born."[65]

English contributions to the Texas farming frontier were not inconsiderable despite relatively small numbers of individuals. The English in Texas, for example, were among the first to use prairie land for farming, not simply as pasture for their livestock. Unlike the native American, they had no taste for clearing thick woodlands, and they did not share the native belief that land that did not grow trees could not grow crops. Before they had time to acquire the American mistrust of prairies, the British immigrants had responded to their natural beauty and broken them to the plow. Thus the west Texas plains proved an asset to the adaptation of British immigrants to Texas farming, and the British proved to the Texans that cotton and wheat could be grown in great abundance from soils previously thought sterile.[66]

In reference to the English settlers in Wharton County, the *Texas Sun* editorialized, "They are true heroes, fighting daily the battle of progress, and making for themselves happy and independent homes. Their names will be inscribed on the pages of our state's history as the people who made this section 'blossom as the rose.' "[67] This tribute might well serve as the epitaph for all English men and women who made the perilous voyage to Texas in the early 19th century and remained to enrich the state.

Chapter 4
Cowboys and Englishmen

For Texas the Civil War was the greatest watershed event since the revolt against Mexico. Although Texas was largely spared the invasion of Union armies and the attendant destruction visited upon her sister states of the Confederacy, losses in Texas manpower and resources were devastating. Thousands of Texan soldiers died on the battlefields of Virginia, Tennessee and Georgia; the system of slave labor on which Texas's cotton-based economy had depended was abolished with the Confederate defeat; and with so many Texans fighting in Southern armies east of the Sabine, the fierce Comanches took a full measure of revenge against the encroaching Anglo-American frontier, driving it back to the east as much as a hundred miles between 1861 and 1865.

The English Texans showed valor and shared hardship in these years alongside their neighbors. Although the majority of the English were devoted followers of the abolitionist cause, those of their number who immigrated to homes in the American South most often mitigated their views to correspond more closely with those of their native-born neighbors.

Amelia Barr, for example, lists among her husband's "prejudices" an "unreasonable detestation of slavery." Although Robert Barr "would not allow that under any circumstances it could be right," his wife was convinced that if he had been compelled to deal with the "thieving, lying, and laziness" of their kitchen help as she did, "his pity for their condition would have been much modified."[1]

During the period of the republic the British press had urged the abolition of slavery as a prime incentive for emigration to Texas. "We write on the presumption," read one such editorial, "that the people of Texas look upon slavery as an evil which it is desirable to rid themselves of, and which the want of sufficient white-labour alone prevents them from abolishing."[2] The Englishman who came to Texas, however, not only learned that Negro emancipation was not desired by the planter society but soon adopted the views of the Texan society himself. Isolated from a community of abolitionist thought and activity, the immigrants in most cases quickly conformed to the views of the slaveholders and quite often acquired slaves of their own.[3]

Robert H. Williams, the son of a London clergyman, is an example. Although intended by his family for the Church, Williams went to sea as a midshipman at the age of 17 but gave up the life of a sailor after only a few voyages as "too staid, too quiet" for his restless

Robert H. Williams, 1863

blood. Neither the merchant marine, the army nor the East Indian service suited him, so he made his mind to "fare forth to the West and the backwoods of the Great Republic."

Settling briefly in western Virginia in 1858, Williams accepted three young Negroes in payment for a debt and so became "that most wicked, cruel monster, a slave-owner!" The stigma of ownership did not rest heavily upon Williams, however, for he soon enjoyed the affection of his chattels and the status which the Old South accorded the slave owner. The possession of Negroes, he quickly learned, "raised me to at least the fringe of aristocracy."

Slave auction

Tiring of the settled life of the East, Williams moved on to the Kansas territory, then the edge of the American frontier and a hotbed of turmoil over the question of whether slavery should be expanded into the western territories. For months Kansas raged with guerrilla fighting between pro- and anti-slavery factions—a prelude to the greater Civil War to come—and Williams's sympathies were "strongly on the side of the South." Joining a company of partisan rangers, he was promoted to the rank of sergeant and then to second lieutenant, and fought in many small but bitter encounters against anti-slavery "Jay Hawkers."

As Kansas began to fill with free-soil partisans, Williams moved south to Texas, where he bought a ranch on the Frio River some 50 miles west of San Antonio. At Texas's secession he volunteered for the army and for the next four years "saw a good bit of fighting here and there, under the 'Lone Star' flag."[4]

Williams was not the only English immigrant brought to a fuller identification with his adopted homeland by Texas's secession. As a New Orleans newspaper observed in 1861, even the normally aloof English "have come forward en masse" to join the Confederate armies. The editor found it remarkable that although some had been in the South but a month or two, the immigrants sided "heart and hand" with Dixie. "Although Englishmen never become American citizens," he observed, "now that there is real work possibly, if not in prospect," they rally to the defense of their new country.[5] Discussing the prospect of war and their wisest course for the future, the Barrs, in common with the entire English community in Austin, decided to remain in Texas. "I like the people," declared Robert Barr, "and I like the country. I am willing to share its fortune, war or peace."[6]

Robert Williams was present at the surrender of General David Twiggs to Texan forces at San Antonio, took part in the capture of the Union garrison at Camp Verde, participated in the battle of the Nueces and tried in vain to prevent the appalling massacre of prisoners which followed that clash between pro-Confederate Anglo-Texans and Unionist German Texans.

Williams's strongest desire throughout the war was to be transferred to the Virginia front where "Lee and Stonewall Jackson and the rest of our gallant leaders were fighting their heroic battles against such desperate odds." Instead, Williams was commissioned by Governor Pendleton Murrah to raise a company of rangers for frontier service against the Comanches. The raiding bands, says Williams, "were much bolder and more careless than usual, knowing just as well as we did that the frontier was no longer protected by U.S. troops, and that our best young 'braves' had gone to the war."

Checking the raiders was, according to Williams, "a thankless task enough, in which little honour, or glory, was to be gained, but which involved incessant hard work and sleepless vigilance." Extending east to west 500 miles from the Brazos to the Nueces and Frio rivers and northward from the Rio Grande for 700 miles, the territory which Captain Williams's 80 rangers were charged with defending was far too vast. At best the soldiers could establish camps near the most exposed ranches and hope to intercept war parties entering the area of white settlement. "All of that autumn and winter [1864]," Williams recalled, "not only we but all the other frontier rangers, almost lived in the saddle, and still could not effectively protect the lives of the ranchers and their property from the ubiquitous Indians."

Numerous English Texans such as Williams put aside personal concerns to strike a blow for the Southern cause, a cause which they did not doubt to be "a sacred one," or that "the Southern States were justified in resisting to the death the oppression of the North."[7]

Confederate camp near Fort Clark, 1861

Reciprocally, Confederate Texas continued its traditional admiration for Great Britain and maintained hope, as it had in the days following the first battles with Mexico, that "the grandmother country" would intervene in favor of Texas freedom. Colonel Fremantle, perfectly sympathetic to the Southern cause and quite taken by the romance of a war for independence at such long odds, often sought out Texas Rangers in Confederate service. Although their uniforms consisted simply of "flannel shirts, very ancient trousers, jack boots with enormous spurs, and black felt hats ornamented with the 'lone star of Texas,' " the English officer found them "extremely civil" and "quite gentlemanlike in their manners." When Fremantle dined with Confederate officers in Texas, they "nearly always proposed the Queen's health, never failed to pass the highest eulogiums upon her majesty," and were most pleased to hear of "the great sympathy which their gallantry and determination had gained for them in England in spite of slavery."[8]

Although the South received no direct aid from England, many English Texans such as Robert Williams served in the Confederate armies with great distinction. The English Texan to achieve highest rank in Confederate service was Brigadier General Thomas Neville Waul, commander of Waul's Texas Legion. Waul saw action at Vicksburg, Mansfield, Pleasant Hill and Jenkins' Ferry, and, with the surrender of the last Southern soldiers west of the Mississippi, returned to the practice of law in Galveston. Interestingly, General Waul, who lived to the age of 91, always claimed South Carolina rather than England as the place of his birth.[9]

Not all of the English Texans in gray, of course, matched the legend of the stainless host that has grown up around the Confederate army. John Pelham Border, for example, won little honor for himself or his cause as commandant of Camp Ford, a Texas stockade for Union prisoners of war. Coming to Texas as a surveyor in 1835, just in time to join the army of the republic, Border settled in San Augustine where

John Pelham Border

he became a prosperous planter. With the secession of Texas in February 1861, he raised a regiment for Confederate service which he led as colonel until assigned to duty at Camp Ford. There his charges variously described him as "an Englishman, a monarchist, and 'a drunken lieutenant-colonel.'" According to more than one Union officer present, he treated a few of the inmates "with surly civility, but the great majority with brutal cruelty."[10]

With few exceptions, English Texan women and children supported the Southern cause with even stronger enthusiasm than the men under arms and suffered privation nearly as great. Amelia Barr, her daughter remembers, "was a Confederate from a to z."[11] In addition to writing stirring patriotic articles for the Austin newspaper, she spent her few spare hours ruling paper and making envelopes for use in the comptroller's office. She lamented, nevertheless, the lack of shoes, cloth, soap, candles and most types of food, and lived in "terror of a slave insurrection." When her son was born in 1863 "not an inch of flannel" could be purchased to make his "barrow coats," but this want was

Amelia Barr, 1880

supplied by an English neighbor who donated his own shirts. Tea also was almost impossible to come by, and one of Lillie Barr's clearest memories is of her mother gathering and drying "Upon" [sic] leaves for her afternoon high tea.[12]

Although beset by genuine poverty, the Barrs cheerfully made do with all manner of ersatz products for the good of the Confederacy. "Corn pone, jonny cakes, and hoe cake" took the place of white bread; and when Mrs. Barr, "a passionate Whist player," wore out her last deck, she painted "a very respectable pack of playing cards."[13] Only on one occasion was a member of the family known to resent a sacrifice made for the cause. Lillie Barr had a pet turkey hen named Nellie that she had raised "from a weakly poult" and fed from the best on her plate. "I loved that turkey as devotedly as a boy loved his dog," she later wrote. When General John B. Magruder, commander of all Confederate forces in Texas, visited Austin, Mrs. Barr sent Nellie for the general's dinner. When young Lillie found her turkey gone, her "grief was perhaps unreasonable, certainly unpatriotic." Her mother had thought that she would have been proud to contribute her pet to "so brave a soldier." Not she! Lillie promptly went into the cornfield and prayed "if that man ate my Nellie, to let a bone choke him, and if he went back to the war, to let some Yankee kill him with a bayonet."[14]

With the war's end the entire family felt a deep grief for "the poor country. My heart aches for Texas," wrote Mrs. Barr, "subjugated and all lost."[15] Fortunately, the Union army of occupation was generally well disposed toward the former rebels. "There was no disorder, and the troops quietly took possession of Austin," remembers Lillie Barr, "behaving in a courteious [sic] manner to all, as far as I ever heard." Because the Barr home lay almost within the Union encampment, the commander of the regiment posted a guard on their porch lest the family be harassed by the soldiers. Lillie remembers that one Englishman was frequently on duty, "a real cockney," who would ask Mrs. Barr to play and sing "The Land of Our Birth." The soldier was apparently unashamed of his tears as the English lady sang:

> Lives there the man with soul so dead
> Who never to himself hath said,
> "This is my own, my native land."[16]

Despite the guard and the courteous treatment, Mrs. Barr was "in terror of the negroes" whom she believed "were going to-and-fro in the darkness, seeking whom they could injure or rob." The Texas economy was also in a panic. Austin's Congress Avenue, which Mrs. Barr thought in 1856 to be "the brightest, happiest, most romantic street in the world," had become "a desolate place." Only a few of Austin's stores remained open, she wrote, and on the day in 1866 that she left the city forever, not more than 12 men and two women "robed in deepest black, and their faces closely covered by long black veils," were visible on the once-crowded street. Moving to formerly prosperous Galveston where financial prospects would perhaps be brighter, the Barrs found the Strand, the principal business street, "rank with waving grass." Warehouses, shops, wharves and public buildings were closed, and all had the air of "hopeless silence and abandonment."[17]

Not all English Texans were equally impoverished by the costly war and the fall of the Confederate government, and those in positions of wealth tended to help their less fortunate neighbors. At the close of the war one Englishman, Fred Carleton, helped to organize the John Bell Hood Camp of Confederate Veterans in Austin. A distinguished lawyer, judge and legislator, Carleton formed the Hood Camp for the purpose of raising means "to acquire land and provide adequate and comfortable quarters for impoverished Confederate veterans." Himself

Confederate Veterans' Home, Austin

a veteran of four years' service in Walker's Division, this prominent Austin citizen lived to see the handsome Confederate Veterans' Home completed and occupied in 1884.[18]

Most Confederate veterans, however, had neither the luxury of Carleton's law practice nor of an old soldiers' home to fall back on. With the cotton kingdom lying desolate at the war's end, many former planters and farmers from east Texas looked west to the plains to secure their futures. If the war had destroyed cotton as the basis for the Texas economy, it had also created a tremendous market for beef in northern cities. By the war's end, wrote Robert Williams, "I was heartily sick of Texas and its roughing, and was longing for a peep of the 'Old Country.'" Unfortunately Williams had been financially ruined by the war and could not afford the trip home. His only resource was his cattle, for which there was no Texas market. In the North, however, "the demand was brisk and the price was good." In 1868, therefore, Williams set out on a trail drive—one of the first to leave postwar Texas, and perhaps the first ever led by an Englishman.[19] Following the end of the war, the population of the United States increased in huge increments, with no increase in numbers of livestock to keep pace. Thus the value of cattle rose rapidly, doubling and then tripling within a few seasons. Texas range cattle, worth less than $10 in 1860, were eagerly bought up by beef-starved northern packing plants at double this price in 1870, and by 1880 range cattle were selling at as much as $30 per head.[20]

Just as cattle raising was becoming truly profitable in Texas, the state's immense northwest quarter was opened to the stockman. Since the discovery in 1870 of a practical process for tanning buffalo hides, buffalo hunters had been making significant inroads into the vast herds on the Texas Panhandle previously the exclusive domain of the Indian. The Comanche, with their Kiowa and Cheyenne allies, saw that the destruction of the buffalo would mean the end of their way of life and so furiously struck back at the intruders. One of the largest Indian war parties ever assembled swept out of the western part of present-day Oklahoma in the spring of 1874 to destroy the buffalo hunters. Zeal and numbers proved no match for European organization and technology, however, for at the Second Battle of Adobe Walls, fought on June 27, 1874, a group of 28 white hunters armed with the new Sharp's buffalo rifle, turned back with heavy losses an assault by 700 Plains Indians led by Quanah Parker.[21] Three months later, at Palo Duro Canyon, Colonel Ranald Mackenzie's 4th U.S. Cavalry surprised rem-

Buffalo hunters' camp

nants of the Kiowas and the Comanches and, although inflicting few casualties, destroyed the Indians' encampment with their vital winter supplies and, more important, their entire herd of 1,424 horses.[22] Left afoot without food or shelter, the fierce Panhandle winter soon drove the last of the hostile tribes into reservations beyond the Texas border, thus ending 40 years of bitter warfare between the Comanches and the Anglo-American Texans and opening the Panhandle to settlement by ranchers and farmers.

Simultaneously with the boom in the Texas cattle industry and the opening of the millions of acres of Panhandle rangeland came a tremendous interest within Great Britain in overseas investment. The industrial revolution and its attendant profits had created a surplus of funds in England, and the maturing of the home economy offered paler prospects for the investment of that surplus. British capital soon found its way into new enterprises in Australia, New Zealand, South Africa, the Far East and Latin America, but no region of the globe received more English attention or more English money than the American West. English pounds were invested in a wide variety of concerns—railroads, mining, industry and public utilities—but land and cattle companies were particular favorites.[23]

Before the Civil War the largest part of British interest in Texas had been among the lower and middle orders of society, eager to immigrate to a new land, there to find more favorable opportunities for themselves and their families. Post-Civil War interest in Texas was keenest among the wealthier strata of society, anxious for new fields in which to invest their capital. Only of secondary importance to them was Texas as a potential area in which to locate second sons—those who by England's laws of primogeniture would inherit nothing of their families' estates but nevertheless had to be provided for as befitted their status as gentlemen.

Always quick to provide information—and misinformation—to any interested readership, the British press soon began issuing descriptions of the Lone Star State in numerous newspapers and magazines. From these periodicals many members of the investing class formed an interest in the cattle industry, and by them were many badly deceived. As late as 1885, for example, one source stated unconditionally that "there is not the slightest element of uncertainty in cattle-raising."[24]

Texas, of course, was delighted to receive both the men and money that England began to pour into its war-ravaged economy and its vacant western territory. The removal of the Comanches from the Panhandle in 1874 opened an immense expanse of free grass, and with beef prices going ever higher, the opportunity for tremendous profits arose for those bold enough to venture onto the Great Plains. Technological advances, too, expanded the market for Texas beef. With new techniques in transportation, refrigeration, packing and canning, meat could now be shipped without deterioration over great distances. For the first time fresh American beef began to offer serious competition to domestic beef in Great Britain.[25] In 1878, 35,000 beeves were shipped from the United States to England, and the following year saw this figure leap dramatically to 71,794. Thus such inventions as refrigerated steamers and railroad cars gave tremendous impetus to investment in land and livestock in Texas.

Texans, on the eve of the cattle boom, still were suffering from the problem, chronic since the days of the revolution, of being "land rich and money poor." The devastation of the Civil War and Reconstruction drained such little capital as the state had been able to accumulate, making Texans quite willing to deed over to English investors their cattle and lands. They were especially willing to sell to capitalists who would pay premium prices for unseen merchandise, and who were willing to

Texas beef for English markets

hire former owners and their employees at wages undreamed of on American-owned ranches. Texas's adjutant general, W.H. King, declared in 1881 that the state was eager to "induce enterprising men with capital from abroad to come in and assist in filling up our waste places and building up many industries."[26]

Texans incorporated in order to "promote immigration to Texas, to facilitate the sale and settlement of lands by immigration, and to introduce laborers, skilled operators and capital" from England.[27] English interests set up companies to investigate the potential for investment in Texas lands as well. In 1877, for example, the *Scotsman* magazine sent its agricultural expert to Texas where he found great opportunity in cattle ranching. In his view, ranching was a simple venture, requiring little money and less work. "The animals get no food," he informed his readers, "summer or winter, but what they gather on the prairies and in the woods; and scarcely any watch is kept over them except in spring or fall, when the increase of the herd is branded."[28] Two years later the British Parliament sent two of its members, Clare Sewell Read and Albert Pell, to Texas to investigate the cattle industry as a potential field for investment. These two individuals spent three months in America and reported to their colleagues that an annual profit of 33⅓ percent was ordinarily made in ranching.[29]

With such glowing, if exaggerated, reports coming to England from America, by 1888 at least 33 companies were registered in Great Britain for the purpose of investing in western ranchland. British capital in Texas cattle enterprises totaled $37 million, of which some $20 million was actually transferred to the United States. At this time English and Scottish companies owned, leased or mortgaged 15 to 20 million acres of northwest Texas—at least 10 percent of the entire state. With British capital came British management to the Texas Panhandle, and with it a clash of cultures.

Capital, in the decades following the American Civil War, was not England's only surplus commodity. As one English observer remarked, "our most pressing needs just now are meat and an outlet for our boys."[30] The highly influential *Blackwoods Edinburgh Magazine* commented on the many instances of the self-made millionaire in America and took the stance that "it is conclusively proved that America must be the place for our superfluous youth. What more can a parent or guardian do, to ensure the future prosperity of their ward," it rhetorically asked, "than to send him there?" Middle-class youths were too often unprepared for a profession, the magazine observed; "Office work is distasteful, and idleness impossible." Thus, it counseled, "our ingenuous youth is to be packed off."[31]

Many of the young men of England were not averse to being "packed off" to the American West. As *MacMillan's Magazine* reported in 1883, "they are tired to death of the confinement of an office . . . their prospects in England are not good, and . . . life 'out west' promises more room for their energies, and a free out-of-door existence as well."[32]

Much of the British image of Texas sprang from the pens of a group of English novelists who chose as their setting the American West and as their theme the conquest of the wilderness by the bold Anglo-Saxon race. By the beginning of the 1870's the "Westerns" of Mayne Reid and Robert M. Ballantyne had joined those of James Fenimore Cooper in displacing in popularity the works of Walter Scott and Charles Dickens, and this popularity was to increase with succeeding generations.

All of the heroes of the English Westerns were "unabashedly British lads who never forsook the King's English or their country's ways." As cultural historian Ray Allen Billington points out in his analysis of the idea of the West in the European mind, the English hero of the Western novel always retains his public school dialect,

delivering such lines as, " 'By jove, I thought my last hour had come,' or assuring grizzled trappers that there was nothing like a good cup of tea out in the wilds to put new life in one."[33]

Significantly, the characters in these adventure novels were determined to return to England after making their fortunes in the West. If all goes well, one such fictional Englishman remarks, he will "return in two or three years with ample means to live once more in dear old England." This trend in fiction followed and surely influenced the demographic trend of the second half of the 19th century. Unlike the movements of whole families to the east Texas farming frontier of antebellum days, the greatest number of English immigrants to Texas after 1865 were single men, intent upon acquiring a fortune and returning home. The ideal of becoming an independent farmer was replaced by the dream of overnight riches with no commitment to the United States as a permanent place of residence. Indeed, by 1880 less than 10 percent of Englishmen coming to America expressed an intention of remaining as farmers.[34]

Through the 1870's and 1880's Englishmen came to Texas in hope of recuperating a lost fortune; they were "wayward sons" sent away from home to learn the virtues of hard work and common sense; they were second sons of noble houses; and, often, they were hard-eyed businessmen, hungry for land and profits.[35] In Texas, one exulted, "there is no trouble about title, deeds, surveyors, and lawyers; possession is nine points of the law, and the tenth is that ever-present law-maker and law-breaker, the Colt revolver."[36] To these men the great frontier was no nostalgic reminder of Nature's glories but a vault of resources to be opened and exploited by the relentless Anglo-American civilization. Material progress was paramount, and Indians and the wilderness were but secondary considerations if they were thought of at all.[37]

The earliest English involvement in the Texas cattle industry had come in the 1840's when Jones and Company established a "beef factory" on the banks of the Trinity near the town of Liberty. These English entrepreneurs bought steers on the hoof at 4¢ a pound and processed them for shipment to Europe. Into an upright iron cylinder would be dumped the equivalent of two barrels of beef. The cylinder then was sealed and the air evacuated by a vacuum process, after which the meat was immersed in strong brine. After one hour's soaking the meat was removed and packed in barrels of coarse salt. From Liberty the barrels of salt meat were sent down river to Galveston to be loaded aboard sailing vessels bound across the Atlantic.

Wasting no part of the steer, Jones and Company also operated a tanning yard to utilize the hides, a candle factory for the tallow and a neat's foot oil bottling plant for the byproduct of the hooves. They also kept a store, selling "family necessities." All cattle were paid for with good English gold.[38]

As the livestock industry in Texas grew, English involvement grew with it, but before cattle became king on the post-Civil War frontier, both native Texans and their English guests made an attempt at large-scale sheep and goat ranching. Among the pioneers of the Texas wool and mutton industry were the Adams brothers, William and Robert, who sailed to Corpus Christi in 1852. During the Civil War the two had accumulated some capital hauling cotton across the south Texas desert to sell or trade at Matamoros. By 1867 they were able to buy cheap land along Barbon Creek in what is now Jim Wells County and to establish a sheep-raising business.

Then a howling wilderness subject to Comanche, Apache and Mexican bandit depredation, the Adams ranch began operation with 8,000 head of sheep which by 1879 had grown to a herd of more than a million. The Adamses at first drove their sheep to market a thousand miles away in Chicago where they sold at $2.00 per head for mutton. Within ten years, however, they had helped to make Corpus Christi the world's greatest wool market, annually shipping ten million pounds of fleece.

Excellent judges of livestock, the Adams brothers became interested in cattle ranching because of their neighbor Richard King of the Santa Gertrudis Ranch, and in 1887 fenced their land and became breeders of fine cattle. They brought some of the first Durham bulls to Texas, and although many died, eventually this fine English breed took precedence over the Texas Longhorns.[39]

Before the transition in English interest from sheep to cattle, however, scores of young Englishmen sailed to Texas in hope of making their fortunes as sheep or goat ranchers. Several of these gentlemen, sorely disillusioned by their experience, wrote lengthy letters to English journals, describing the hardships of life on a western sheep ranch and bemoaning the impossibility of rising above the lowly status of shepherd. One such aspiring sheep baron who had been "accustomed to call himself a 'gentleman,'" lamented the utter isolation of the sheepherder from the rest of mankind. "North, south, and west stretch the rolling prairies, broken only by the mesas," he wrote, "the rocky sides of which give shelter to the wolves, bears, and pumas" that thrived on the sheep ranching frontier. Such a setting dictated for the shepherd "a peaceful, though lonely and dreary life," he warned potential immigrants.[40]

Sheepherders' camp, 1892

Dugout cabin, Matador Ranch, c. 1908-1910

As for his home in the West, the gentleman stockman enjoyed a dugout, "a small hut partly built above ground with logs chinked with mud," so named because it was partially dug out of a hill. One correspondent to an English journal described the typical dugout as six feet square in size with a flat board roof covered with earth. An old stovepipe was pushed through one corner of the roof "and called by courtesy a chimney."[41]

For furniture this son of English aristocracy could boast one three-legged stool and two blankets. His pillow was his coat and vest and, "if the night is very warm and sheep are quiet," his trousers. Accustomed at home to china, silver and crystal, his utensils now consisted of a tin dish, an iron pot, a long-handled spoon, a frying pan, a coffee pot, a tin plate and cup, a little-used fork and "the all-useful, indispensable 'butcher-knife.' "[42]

Although brought up in broadcloth and fine linen, this erstwhile dandy described himself as "only a sunburnt face very much begrimed with dust and perspiration." He had exchanged his tailor-made suits for a faded blue flannel shirt, coarse brown canvas trousers—"so stained and discolored by grease and dirt as to be almost black"—clumsy, ill-fitting shoes and an old felt hat "that only by great exercise of imagination could one fancy had ever been white."[43]

Worst of all was the work. "The first thing brought before your notice out west," writes another disgruntled correspondent, "is that a man has all the women's work to do as well as his own." Much to his disgust he learned that he was expected to light the fire, cook, wash dishes, cut firewood and draw water, "in fact, do all the worst drudgery," in addition to the tending of his ovine charges.

Herding, he commented, which *"looks* so easy and pleasant," actually entailed hard work and much physical discomfort. In addition to the isolation, monotony, hunger, thirst, heat and rain in which the herders labored, the management of the sheep was a major chore. To keep a restless flock from racing to its corral during the last hour before sundown while in sight of his cabin, from which there was already wafting toward him the "incense of supper," the gentleman shepherd considered "as good a test of what stuff a man is made of as I know."[44]

Very few were the young men who achieved the dream with which they had left their English homes. Usually a single season of sheep tending sufficed to disillusion the aspirant stockman and to send him back to England or the East. "One by one, all our previous hopes as to western life have faded away; all the novelty of your work has gone; everything that seemed worth living for has departed from your life," a failed rancher wrote to *MacMillan's.*[15] Yet English pluck was strong. Even in the wake of a disastrous career as a sheep rancher, one high-spirited Englishman reported, "It was glorious fun, like pic-nics always."[46]

Sheep ranch, 1892

While south central Texas saw cattle take over the land once roamed by thousands of English-owned sheep, goats remained on the Edwards Plateau, making south central Texas one of the great goat-raising areas of the world. Ninety-seven percent of the United States' mohair comes from Texas, and most of the Texas production comes from Terrell, Crockett, Valverde, Edwards and surrounding counties.[47]

Much more to the taste of the upper- and upper-middle-class English youth than the life of a shepherd was that of a cowboy. Young Englishmen came to Texas in droves, carrying with them a thirst for adventure and the illusion, fostered by the British press, that a cattle rancher had only to build a fence. "This done," intoned the *Anglo-American Times*, "native cattle with improved bulls should be turned in; the [rancher] would have no other trouble with them than branding the increase each year."[48]

The English gentry took to cowpunching as it never did to following the plough. By the mid-1880's young British university graduates from upper-class families commonly came to Texas for a year or two as cowboys in order to learn the cattle business and to satisfy a lust for adventure.

Frank Collinson, for example, grew up in a typically middle-class home in Yorkshire. His parents were sympathetic and intelligent, and when his mother received a letter from Captain Story, a relative living in Texas, they readily understood how the teenaged boy could become inflamed with fantasies of western adventure. Captain Story had fought under Sam Houston at San Jacinto, owned a wagon yard in San Antonio and had an interest in a stage line. There were many cattle and horse ranches in that part of Texas, the letter related, and plenty of opportunities for a young man willing to rough it on the frontier.

Realizing, perhaps, that it was hopeless to try to keep him in "old and weary England" when his "blood called for a new and untamed country," his parents at last bought Frank's fare to Galveston.

Working first as a cowboy for Judge George H. Noonan on a horse ranch near Castroville, Collinson's career included driving cattle, fighting Indians, hunting buffalo—experiencing "every adventure that would appeal to a red-blooded youth"—and at last writing fictional and autobiographical accounts of life on the Texas frontier.[49] Collinson has been characterized as "the most outstanding English cowboy who ever came to America and one of the most wonderful storytellers the Old West has ever produced." J. Frank Dobie paid him the tribute of identifying him as "one of the most powerful men I ever met" and one who "ranged as far west as the grass grew."[50]

Unlike the native American and the London-based investor in western lands, the young Englishman who came to Texas to be a cowboy had a mystic respect for the land and its traditions. Americans, who had erased the eastern wilderness with smoke and plow, were quite proud of the civilization that they had created in its place. The plains to them were but a new area to subdue and to exploit. To the adventure-seeking English lad, fresh from public school and full of notions of romance and glory, the American West was, like Peter Pan's "Never-Never Land," the setting for a fantasy life come true and a locale which must always remain changeless.[51]

When faced with the actuality of life on the open range among the wild native Texans, many an English lad recoiled in horror, but many others took naturally to the life of the cowboy. It was J. Frank Dobie's belief that "the greatest happiness possible to a man . . . is to become civilized . . . and then . . . to live in a wilderness . . . with a few barbarians to afford picturesqueness and human relations." Many young English gentlemen of the 19th century shared this view, and found Texas the ideal wilderness and the cowboy the perfect barbarian.[52]

The image of the American cowboy presented in English fiction was one of virtue, honesty and decorum. This picture was vastly appealing to the younger sons of noble English houses seeking their fortunes in the West and to English schoolboys in quest of adventure. Once in Texas they attempted to live up to the idealized portrait of the cowboy and to a remarkable degree succeeded in doing so. Not only did they exhibit the qualities of pluck and valor for which the Victorian Englishman was world renowned, but their riding skills, perfected while fox hunting, gained them the respect of the hard-riding Texans. Knowing that life on the plains was but an interlude in their lives, these well-bred English gentlemen thought of their lives as cowboys as an irresistible lark. "I know as well as anyone," wrote one English devotee of the adventurous life of a cowboy, "that to a hot-blooded English boy, roughing it, and facing dangers which he just manages to overcome, are fun and frolic."[53]

Some English gentlemen, of course, preferred to acquire their ration of adventure and experience in livestock ranching in a more or less sanitary environment. Byron Van Raub, an enterprising Englishman, sensed this need and built Texas's first "dude ranch" just north of Leon Springs. Offering "practical education as cow-men" to those of his countrymen "who contemplated or were desirous of going into the live-stock business," Van Raub prospered on his ranch, his principal stock being the numerous "young men of means" who flocked to him at $1,200 a year.[54]

Others, however, plunged directly into the heart of the Texas frontier without friends, experience or even a sure knowledge of their physical location. One young man wrote to *Cornhill* of his first Texas adventure: "I found myself, after a fortnight's continuous travel, and before I had fully realized the fact over five thousand miles away from home and friends, in the sordid, reeking saloon of a small prairie settlement, surrounded by a motley crew of bullwhackers, muleskinners, graingers [sic], drummers, gamblers, and cow-boys, the latter easily distinguishable by their devil-may-care air and fantastic get-up. In these unwonted surroundings I am not ashamed to confess that I was overcome by a feeling of complete isolation."[55]

Few English lads, finding themselves in such circumstances, panicked, however, and most soon made a place for themselves in the rough-and-tumble communities which they had crossed half the world to seek. During his first months on a Dumas, Texas, ranch, John Edgar of Durham reported to the Newcastle *Chronicle* that he had "with more or less success (chiefly the latter some will say) been trying to master the mysteries of cattle, and hog culture." Although not so far advanced in his studies as he would have liked, Edgar fancied that he had made some progress, now being able to "distinguish a horse from a cow, and observe a slight difference between a sheep and a hog."[56]

The young English gentleman, spending his season rusticating on a Texas ranch, was fascinated by the native cowboy. Predisposed to idealize his new colleagues by the image presented in the English press, few English cowboys disputed the claim of their American comrades to a sensitive pride, an aggressive spirit of independence, a keen intelligence and a set of "sportsman-like" instincts. English journalists on the Texas frontier noted with admiration the total absence of the cringing servility which was the byproduct of generations of rigid class distinction in the older civilizations of Europe.[57]

The proud tradition of freedom and self-reliance had its darker side as well, which the English were quick to remark. The cowboy could be "shockingly cruel, hasty in temper, and unbridled in tongue." In no setting was this unfortunate side effect of liberty more pronounced than

A Texas cowboy

in Texas.[58] As one English commentator observed, "Cowboys can be divided into two classes: those hailing from the Lone Star State, Texas, the other recruited from Eastern States." The Texans, he recorded, were unrivaled in horsemanship, hardihood, and skill with rope and gun.[59] Colonel Fremantle had been wonderfully impressed by the Texas horseman's ability to catch steers by the tail while at full gallop and to "throw them by slewing them around." The Texans' ability to pick small objects from the ground or to shoot jack rabbits with a revolver while riding at full speed were equally awesome to the visiting soldier. The only drawback was their wild reputation.[60] "The others," he notes, "are less able but more orderly men." The Texans' reputation stems from their "excitable tempers," a trait which causes them always to be "on the shoot—that is, very free in the use of their revolvers."[61]

In the manner of their speech, as well, the cowboy proved shocking to his gently reared English auditors. "Never before had I heard such swearing and cursing, such blasphemous meaningless oaths and mighty anathemas." Despite their "rough and uncouth manner and speech," most Englishmen found their Texan companions "good fellows all." The hardships, isolation and dangers of the cowboy's life developed "all the sterner manly qualities" that the English so admired.[62]

Some of the softer virtues were included in the composite cowboy, and these, too, touched the English sensibilities. Cold, hungry and weary English travelers on the Texas cattle range seem never to have approached an isolated ranch but that "the best of everything would be offered." One English cowboy recalled with fondness how "the snuggest corner, the warmest blankets" were invariably forced upon him, and how many times his stay extended for days "and yet not a penny would my hosts accept on parting."[63]

The Texas cowboy's courage, his stoic indifference to suffering, his generosity and his dogged industry were virtues unsurpassed in the English value system, and thus the cowboy became and has endured as a British hero of mythic proportions.[64]

However admirable the chivalric though rough cowboy appeared to the youth of England, and however plucky those lads were who came to Texas to try their lot on a cattle ranch, the English adventurer soon learned that "the cow-boy's life is not all beer and skittles." The vision of sport and adventure too soon gave way to "a very hard and not very agreeable reality."[65] English cowboy John Baumann wrote in the *Fortnightly Review* that having lived on the open range and shared the toils and pleasures of the life of a ranch hand, he had

> no hesitation in warning any restless, roving spirits who may be attracted by picturesque descriptions of a cowboy's life that, unless they are prepared to toil during the long summer months, both by day and by night, for small pay on scant fare, to be in the saddle from early dawn until sunset both Sundays and weekends, to abstain from comfort and civilization for the greater part of every year, and so to wear themselves out with exposure and manifold fatigues as to be reckoned old and past their work whilst still young men in years, they had better remain at home and leave cowboy life alone.[66]

Among the hardships which faced the Englishman-turned-rancher were hard weather, hostile Indians, fearsome beasts and reptiles, and no less violent companions and near-fatal food. Texas weather ran the scale from the famous "blue northers" which, with typical British understatement, one dilettante cowpuncher described as " 'bracing' to say the least of it"[67] to the hellish summers for which "the words 'hot' and 'dry' do not convey" a fraction of the meaning to another.[68]

Comanches, cattle rustlers and rattlesnakes made the Colt revolver "the herder's companion, philosopher and friend,"[69] according to Arthur H. Patterson's reminiscence of his life as a Texas cowboy, but a fellow English Texan wrote that he was "happy to say I never knew or heard of an Englishman who thought of throwing up western life on that account."[70]

Perhaps worst of all to the aristocratic Englishman was the utter monotony of the unwholesome frontier diet. Patterson described his daily fare as bacon, *salted, not cured,*" flour, green coffee, black Mexican beans, soda, occasional onions and, "to vary the monotony of the bacon," mutton soaked in brine.[71] Meals of such stuff were tolerable to the young English cowboys only because they knew that their Texas sojourn was only a lark, a year or two of adventure after which they would return to the halls of their ancestors in "dear old England."

To the English lord who came to Texas to stay, however—who had invested heavily in Texas land and cattle and who made a more or less permanent home on the range administering the affairs of the ranch—the cuisine of the cowboy was a source of unremitting woe. Sir

Chuck wagon on the JA Ranch, 1907

Archibald Majoribanks, for example, surely pined for the meals served at Brooke House, his family's London establishment. The endless courses served on bone china and old silver certainly haunted his memory as he sliced into Texas bacon and found it all fat or when a sack of dried prunes contained more worms than prunes. His misery echoes in his letters to the grocer from whom he ordered his ranch's provisions: the supplies, he wrote, were "four-fifths . . . waste" and "utterly unfit for human consumption."[72]

In exchange for his year of adventure and comradeship, the English public school graduate left a small imprint on Texas. One former cowhand recalled, "The Englishman brought a lot of culture to the West." There were but few books on the cattle range, and he seemed always to have a volume of Shakespeare in his saddlebags; "it was the decent thing to do." He read his books aloud to Texas cowboys whose education had never progressed beyond the barest rudiments of reading and writing, and, wondrous to relate, the drovers would sit on their spurs and listen in silence and concentration to *Hamlet* or *King Lear.* One cowboy remarked after hearing a reading of *Julius Caesar,* "That Shakespeare is the only poet I've ever heard who was fed on raw meat."[73]

Less numerous than the English cowboys but equally important to the development of west Texas were the English ranchers who invested not one or two years, but their lives and fortunes in the cattle industry. To these members of the English ruling class a cattle brand became synonymous with a coat of arms, and the ranch equivalent to a barony in the Old Country. Together, these men poured millions of pounds into the badly depressed Texas economy between 1865 and 1890, and together they opened—and owned or leased—virtually the entire Texas Panhandle. The names of their ranches have become legendary, and their blood still courses the veins of the oldest of the region's families.

In terms of sheer size, few English-owned ranches rivaled the XIT. The brand declared the magnitude of its range: XIT stood, according to Panhandle lore, for "ten [counties] in Texas." In 1875 the Texas Legislature set aside three million acres of public lands for the financing of a new capitol building in Austin. These lands, running from Oklahoma down the New Mexico line for 200 miles, were sold in 1885 to the Capitol Freehold Land and Investment Company, Limited, of London. Within three years this company raised £2,000,000 sterling or $15,000,000 by selling debentures to wealthy Englishmen anxious to cash in on the American cattle boom. Directed by such worthies as the earl of Aberdeen, the marquis of Tweeddale, the Honorable Lord Thurlow and Henry Seaton-Karr, M.P., the Capitol Syndicate seemed an "exceptionally well-secured and desirable investment."[74]

Perhaps feeling themselves too ignorant of the ways of Texas ranching to effectively manage the XIT, the syndicate's Board of Directors left the administration of the ranch and its 150,000 head of cattle to the Texans. Colonel B.H. "Barbecue" Campbell was appointed general manager of the XIT, and Berry Nations, also a west Texas native, became range foreman. Of the half dozen senior officials on the XIT, only one, Walter S. Maud, was English. Universally acclaimed as "a jolly good fellow," Maud was "unversed in the ways of the range, but not at all overburdened by responsibilities." XIT historian J. Evetts Haley has recorded that "between drinking highballs at the ranch and gambling in Tascosa, he really put in full time."[75]

Unfortunately for the company's owners, the XIT never prospered as a cattle-raising enterprise with bad weather, theft and poor management depleting the company's herds. As property values rose after the turn of the century, the syndicate was able to liquidate its debt, however, by selling farmsteads from its three-million-acre domain.

By 1912 the last of the XIT cattle were sold, and little remained to remind the region of the English contribution to its development. English pounds, however, had enabled Texas to build its fine new capitol in 1888, and the ranch's policy of herd improvement brought some of the first Hereford, Shorthorn and Angus bulls to Texas to fatten and tenderize the hardy native Longhorn range stock, a major benefit to the Texas cattle industry.[76]

Other English capitalists purchased the 187,000-acre LX Ranch and its 40,000 cattle in 1884 for £91,727. This Panhandle establishment was comprised of portions of Randall, Potter, Carson, Moore and Hutchison counties, and could be considered small only in comparison with the giant XIT. The LX's new proprietors, the American Pastoral Company of London, sent English foremen to supervise the ranch, a procedure which caused a great deal of friction between the English managers and their Texas cowboys. English management on the LX was unable to save it from the fate of the XIT, it too losing money annually to Texas droughts, freezes and desperadoes.[77]

Another famous Panhandle ranch under British ownership was the JA Ranch of John G. Adair. Adair, son of a wealthy British family, had come to America in 1866 to open a brokerage firm in New York. Caught up by the general fascination for the West, Adair journeyed to Kansas for a buffalo hunt in 1874 where he killed no buffalo but did succeed in shooting a horse from under himself. Despite his demonstrated ineptitude in the skills of a cowboy, Adair remained in the West and moved his family to Denver the following year. There he met the legendary Charles Goodnight, and together they purchased and stocked the JA Ranch near the Palo Duro Canyon. Adair made but three trips to his ranch, leaving the management to the abundantly qualified Goodnight. Thus English money and Texas management eventually turned a 1,500-head, 2,500-acre ranch into one of more than 100,000 cattle and 1⅓ million acres in Armstrong, Briscoe, Donley, Hall, Randall and Swisher counties by 1903.

The second generation of Adairs took to the cattle culture little better than the first. James Wadsworth, Adair's nephew and a U.S. Senator from New York, was nominal ranch manager from 1912 to 1915, but in fact spent only slightly more time on it than had his uncle. In 1945 the ranch came under the management of Montgomery Wadsworth Richie, Adair's stepgrandson. The son of an English mother and an American father, Richie, like most other third-generation Englishmen in Texas, has shed his English identity, and, although he maintains European ties, rightly considers himself to be thoroughly American.[78]

JA Ranch headquarters, 1907

The Rowe Ranch, the first in Collingsworth County, was established in 1878 by three brothers of a prominent English family. Under the famous RO brand, this enterprise consisted of 300,000 acres in Donley, Wheeler, Gray and Collingsworth counties and ran 12,000 to 20,000 head of cattle under English management until the sole remaining brother died aboard the S.S. *Titanic* on April 15, 1912.[79]

The Francklyn Land and Cattle Company, one of the earliest and largest cattle ranches established in west Texas, and its successor, White Deer Lands, covered another 640,000 acres of the Panhandle, and a dozen other British-owned companies rounded out almost total control of northwest Texas between 1870 and 1900. In many cases the English owners held the land *in absentia*, hiring Texas foremen and cowboys to work the stock. In such a fashion F. Theodore Cookson lost a $100,000 investment to an unscrupulous general manager.[80]

In other cases, such as that of James Gray of the Moon Ranch, the English owner looked upon the outfit as a sporting proposition more than as a business. Gray's roundup wagon, it was said, could easily be followed by the trail of beer bottles and wild game hides left in its wake. More interested in running their packs of greyhounds, kangaroo hounds and Scotch deerhounds than they were in coping with the monotonous details involved in keeping a cattle ranch operating at a profit, many English sportsmen lost their ranches because of the constant temptation of hunting the many types of wild game which still covered the western prairies in the 1880's.[81]

Perhaps the most notorious of English sportsmen who lost fortunes in Texas is Joseph Heneage Finch, the seventh earl of Aylesford. In his youth a close personal friend of the Prince of Wales, later King Edward VII, Aylesford encountered some embarrassing domestic difficulties in 1883 and immigrated to Texas. Near Big Spring the earl engaged in the ranching business, but the mountain of baggage which accompanied him from England included a carload of purebred horses and

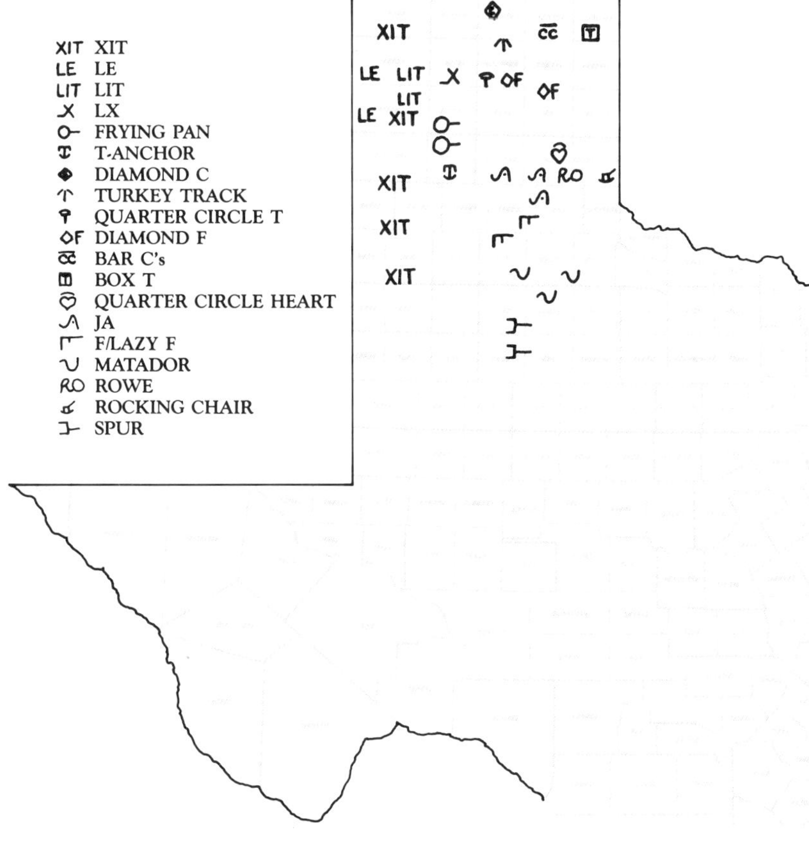

*Heneage Finch, seventh earl
of Aylesford, 1883*

fine dogs. With his Chesterfieldian manners and his English riding togs, Aylesford might have become a laughingstock on the Texas frontier had it not been for his broad camaraderie and his lavish spending. Unimpressed by either his ancient house and lineage or his impressive list of prominent friends, the locals declared, "Look here, Earl, all that stuff don't go down here. We'll just call you 'Judge' "[82]

The "Judge," a title as close to nobility as Big Spring knew, offset the effect of his "muley" English saddle with his generosity as a host. Introduced to his new peers as "a man whom everybody must treat right since they might want to borrow some of his tobacco," Aylesford soon surpassed all expectations. As he was accustomed to living well, he built a hotel on 3rd Street to ensure himself a good room. Because he liked to dine well, he purchased the Big Spring butcher shop so that he would receive the choicest cuts of meat. Appreciating a drink, he bought the town saloon to get his daily supply of whiskey, and all who frequented the establishment were his guests. This was a man whom Texans were happy to claim as one of their own.

But "the Lord God of Aylesford" neglected his ranch to ride to hounds after wolves and coyotes, and his powerful thirst considerably abbreviated his life. At the time of his death in 1885 the estate in which he had invested $40,000 for cattle alone sold for only $750.[83]

Not all English sportsmen in Texas were so prodigal. The Anson brothers of Staffordshire were the sons of the second earl of Lichfield and Lady Georgianna Louisa, daughter of the duke of Abercorn. Their forebears included Lord George Anson, First Lord of the Admiralty; Thomas William Anson, Colonel Commandant of the Queen's Own Royal Staffordshire Yeomanry; and Lieutenant Colonel Henry A. Anson, Member of Parliament and winner of the Victoria Cross. Nevertheless, these young men never presumed on their birthright or on their letters of credit from the bank. Unlike many of their country and rank, they needed no special tutoring in the facts of Texas democracy: that ability, industry, integrity and a pleasant manner were far more valuable than money and Old World social connections.

Just down from Harrow in 1882, 18-year-old Claud was the first of the Ansons to come to Texas. Sent by his family to establish a place for himself and his younger brothers, Claud went first to visit a brother in Canada, then moved on. In Texas he spent two years on the Jim Ned Ranch in Coleman County learning the cattle business before investing his £1,000 inheritance in the Kickapoo Ranch east of San Angelo where he was joined by his brothers Frank and William.

Billy Anson (with banjo), Claud Anson (in rocking chair) and friends at Anson ranch at Valera, Coleman County

William Anson

Billy Anson (far left) on polo field at Valera

William became "Billy" Anson, Texas's "greatest breeder, promoter, and historian of the Quarter Horse."[84]

In England the Ansons had belonged to that social class which looked upon horses and horsemanship as part and parcel of one's existence, and it was only natural that the breeding of the finest horses possible should become a major concern on their ranch. "It was not until the occurrence of the Boer War," William Anson recorded, however, "that the importance of Texas as a horse and mule producing territory was fully realized." With the English invasion of the Transvaal in 1899, the Ansons, who were the nephews of the marquis of Lansdowne, Queen Victoria's Minister of War, received a contract from the British Army to supply remounts. Before the end of hostilities they had shipped to South Africa about 20,000 horses, which they had selected after looking at close to 100,000.[85]

Less profitable to the Ansons but a source of greater pride was their sale of polo ponies to northern and eastern clubs. Expert polo players themselves, the Ansons helped to popularize the sport in Texas and early realized the merit of the quarterhorse as an ideal polo pony. Long valued by the cowboy as the finest breed for working cattle at close quarters, the Ansons immediately recognized in this sturdy Texas animal the stamina, intelligence, quickness of response and sureness of foot required of the mounts of those who play "the sport of kings." So fine were the ponies bred on the Anson ranch, products of English sires and the finest Texas mares, that they often sold for up to $2,500 in New York, Philadelphia and Washington.

Claud Anson, the family pioneer, never lost his loyalty to England and always displayed a portrait of HRH Alexandra, Princess of Wales, in his quarters. In 1901 he married Lady Clodagh de la Poer Beresford, youngest daughter of the sixth marquis of Waterford. Three years later, because his bride found Texas life "too wild and lonesome," they returned to England. Frank remained in Texas till just after the turn of the century, while William stayed on.[86]

Other Englishmen too made good Texans and brought not only much-needed capital but an equally needed offering of refinement to the frontier. Cecil Victor Payne Buckler, for example, came to the Panhandle in 1905 where his new associates were cowboys, "ribald in speech, rough in dress, boisterous in habit." Buckler was accepted by his new peers for his honesty, courage and industry but remained as articulate, concise in speech and immaculate in dress as he had been in prep school at Arundel House in Surrey. In 1914 Buckler dropped "Victor" (for Queen Victoria) from his name and became a United States citizen.[87]

W.E. Busk, owner of the 100,000-acre BSK ranch in Coleman County, was also well liked and respected by his cowboys. When on the ranch he did his full share of the work, and although dignified in manner and commanding in appearance, he was a generous and democratic overseer, taking meals with his men and never forgetting to bring gifts for his regular hands and the foreman's family when returning from England.[88]

Unfortunately, not all English owners understood or appreciated their cowboys, and the cowboys, in return, could make life intolerable for their elitist employers. The Right Honourable Cecil Archibald John Majoribanks of the Rocking Chair Ranche serves as a case in point. Sent from London to manage the ranch owned primarily by his brother, the baron of Tweedmouth, Majoribanks did not care for the land, the work or the Texans, preferring to hunt with his blooded dogs as he had in England.

One Rocking Chair hand remembered the day that the new English manager arrived on the ranch and introduced himself to the cowboys as Sir Archibald Majoribanks. If he expected the cowboys to call him "Sir Archibald," one old-timer recounts, he was greatly mistaken—they called him merely "Marshie" or "Old Marshie," and whether he liked it or not, the name stuck.

To the cowboys of his outfit he was merely another tenderfoot. They judged him, as all outlanders, by their own standards and took him at what he was worth. The "Honourable" was meaningless to them, since they were unfamiliar with the English order of nobility. The greater the airs he affected, the more the border toughs bullied him. The old cowboy recalls that they often "charged down on him at full gallop, yelling like wild Indians," shooting around his feet and head and "cursing till the air was blue," for no reason other than to remind themselves, and him, that they were as good men as the "Honourable Archie."

Needless to say, the Rocking Chair, locally known as "Nobility's Ranch," soon passed into other hands. Although comprised of 150,000 of the best-watered acres in Wheeler and Collingsworth counties, the management soon put the ranch on the rocks. Ironically, it was another Englishman, John Drew, who gained the greatest profit from Baron Tweedmouth's investment. An experienced cattleman, Drew was hired as ranch foreman, and it was he who ran the outfit while Sir Archie was drinking and gambling in Mobeetie. Unfortunately for the Rocking Chair, however, Drew was a thief. Panhandle legend has it that when Tweedmouth came to Texas to inspect his herd, Drew placed him at the foot of a small mesa and ran the same cattle around and around it while the baron counted. Apocryphal or true, the story illustrates the fact that English investors frequently placed vast sums in undertakings that they neither understood nor took an active interest in, and almost invariably they lost their holdings to more energetic if less honest Americans or fellow Englishmen.[89]

Not making the task of the English rancher any easier in Texas was a natural antipathy which existed between the aristocratic English and the democratic Americans. The general American idea of an Englishman was the stage stereotype, a titled fop, vulgarly overdressed, almost invariably wearing white spats, with monocle, walking stick and silk hat. Whatever his class or education he never used "h's" in his speech, and "Don't you know," "deucedly clever" and "blooming" punctuated every sentence.

On the Texas frontier the genuine article proved at least as exotic. Illustrating the fastidious nature of the English gentleman rancher, the Texas cowboys tell of the blistering summer day when the British manager rode into a line camp complaining of a hellish thirst. "How's that?" asks a hand, "You passed a windmill and forded a creek on the way out."

"I didn't have a cup," was the astonished reply.[90]

As George Bernard Shaw once observed, the English language has often been more a divisive than a common factor between its speakers from the two sides of the Atlantic. The story is told, for example, that as a Texas blue norther approached a brace of English peers on an inspection tour of the LX Ranch, a cowboy warned them, "You fellers better hunt for dry; it's gonna rain like hell here in a few minutes."

"What did the fellow say?" one bemused lord inquired of the other one.

"He said the aspects of the elements seem to impend precipitation, and advises us to seek shelter."

"Perhaps we had best return to our quarters. Hi, knave! Assist us to mount!"[91]

Besides the language, table manners — or lack thereof — caused stares of incredulity and wonder across every table which seated both lord and cowboy. During his tour of inspection of the Rocking Chair,

Two views of an English sportsman in the West

Lord Tweedmouth "went democratic" and sat down to dine with his cowboys. The meal had scarcely begun when he adjusted his monocle and remarked to a foreman, "Our cowservants are quite frightfully talented at eating with their knives." Although fascinated by the performance, he could not see the reason for it. "We provide forks, you know."

The foreman explained to his lordship that "some of these boys were grown before they saw a fork," then had more explaining to do, this time to the cowboys, when the meal was finished. "Why does that old buzzard keep lookin' at me through his little peepglass?" they wanted to know. "Lord Tweedmouth meant no offense," he assured them. Rather than "sizing them up for their hide and tallow" as one feared, he was only "admiring the way you can handle beans with a knife."[92]

Other English visitors, not blessed with diplomatic foremen, were made to suffer the consequences of their disdain. On one of his infrequent visits to the JA Ranch, owner John Adair was much affronted

John G. Adair

when one of the hands, uninvited, seated himself at table with him and his lady and began to eat, using his knife as both fork and spoon.

"Really, old chap, we're not accustomed to eating with the servants."

"Here I am, a boy who can ride anything that grows hair, and yet you say I ain't good enough to eat with you folks."

On a night of savage wind and rain the insulted cowboy got his revenge. On roundup Adair slept on a cot in a comfortable, spacious tent. Galloping by on his horse, the "servant" roped the top of Adair's shelter and dragged it off into the stormy night, leaving the British gentleman howling like King Lear.[93]

The Texas cowboy, the son of 200 years of frontier democracy, was no respecter of family crest or inherited wealth. Although blood was seldom spilled over such points of honor, the cowboy very quickly gave the English aristocrat to know that his title and airs were meaningless on the frontier. Often told is the story of the cowboy who jostled an Englishman in a cow town saloon. "Fellow, mind who you are getting up against; I'm the son of a lord," retorted the offended aristocrat. The cowboy threw off his coat and informed him that while he might be the son of a lord in England, he was a son of another sort in America.[94]

This antagonism and incipient violence was to a large degree mitigated by the Texan's broad sense of humor and the Englishman's proverbial sense of fair play. The English gentry, however exalted their position at home, soon learned that their "high rank didn't amount to a whoop" on a cattle ranch. W. Baillie Groham returned to England in the 1890's after a few years of cattle ranching in America and advised Englishmen thinking of following in his footsteps to "do as others do" in Texas. Social equality, he opined, although often having a way of "expressing itself in a very extravagant and disagreeable fashion" is the main factor in the rapid growth and development of the West and must never be disparaged by the Englishman on the frontier. "A man out West is a man," said Groham, "let him be the poorest cowboy he will assert his right of perfect equality with the best of the land, betraying a stubbornness it is vain and unwise to combat." The English gentleman, brought up in a society of rigid class hierarchy, will at first be offended by the cowboys under him, "who by look and manner will let him know that the question of who is the better man of the two has long been settled in his own mind." The lord's hands will itch, Groham predicts, when a curt "do it yourself" is the only response to an order which "the help" deems beneath his dignity. In time, however, the aristocrat will become accustomed to the mores of the frontier, and "if there is no false pride about him, the good points of the English character, to which none are more keenly alive than the free-and-easy Western men, will have gained him not only the good will but the devoted attachment of the reckless characters surrounding him."[95]

The days of the cattle boom in west Texas, though glorious, were brief. By the end of the 1880's smart money was moving elsewhere, and by the mid-1890's most English holdings had been liquidated, often at tremendous loss. Besides mismanagement, the opening of rangeland from Colorado to Canada, the coming of the railroads and the dirt farmer, locoweed, drought, Indians, "Texas fever," wolves, outlaws and prairie fires all contributed to the decline in the value of Texas cattle. In 1887 John Baumann commented in the *Fortnightly Review* that "the boom has passed away, leaving only blank looks and empty pockets."[96]

Losses of the middle 1880's, although discouraging, did not extinguish British interest in west Texas. "No doubt there is money to be made in cattle yet," Baumann predicted, although the days of enormous fortunes rapidly made were no doubt past. The Tascosa *Pioneer* reported in 1888, in fact, that "A whole half-dozen . . . blarsted Britishers . . . have . . . been looking over the Panhandle with a view to purchasing the rest of it."[97]

On April 19, 1890, however, Governor James S. Hogg, in a speech before the Texas Legislature, accused "English Lords, syndicates, and corporations" of enclosing vast estates which they intended eventually to lease to foreign "serfs and peons" who would make a mockery of Texas democracy, voting according to the dictation of the "English aristocracy."[98] Although these conspiracy theories and tirades against foreign involvement were absurd, they were typical of an America in the throes of her most xenophobic period. Nowhere was the suspicion of all things foreign more pronounced than in the states of the old Confederacy, the region of the United States with the most homogeneous Anglo-Celtic population base. This phenomenon manifested itself in part with the emergence of the severe "Jim Crow" legislation, but in west Texas, where Negroes were few and English investors were many, the great national prejudice expressed itself as the Alien Land Law of April 12, 1892. This piece of legislation prohibited the acquisition of land by aliens and required foreign nationals holding land in Texas to dispose of their property or to become United States citizens within ten years. Although ill-advised and only loosely enforced, this law, combined with the depression of the 1890's and the hostility of native farmers and small cattlemen, led to the liquidation of most English holdings in the Panhandle between 1893 and 1896. As Richard Harding Davis observed in 1892, "a record of the failures of the English colonists of good family . . . would make a book, and a very sad one."[99]

With few exceptions profits were small, and in many cases the losses outweighed the gains. The unearned increment was probably the salvation of most English investors, with the rise in Texas land prices taking up the slack produced by the decline in the price of cattle.[100]

Interestingly, even the hostility of Texas's climate and legislature were not sufficient to dry up British capital investment in the Panhandle. United States mortgage banks during this period were charging very high interest rates and were willing to loan money for only very short periods on farms and ranches. The English still had surplus capital, and, since they were prohibited from directly purchasing Texas land, they were willing to make indirect investments in the cattle industry by making long-term, low-interest loans to Texas stockmen. In 1889 alone, the British and American Mortgage Company, Ltd., the Colonial and United States Mortgage Company, Ltd., and the Canadian and American Mortgage Company, Ltd., all were chartered in London to make loans to American farmers and ranchers. Unlike investment companies which bought and managed ranches, mortgage loan companies generally prospered, probably because the bulk of these loans were made to substantial rancher-capitalists who dominated the Texas political and economic scene in the late 19th century.[101]

Although much English money was lost in Texas and many English aristocrats left Texas with only bitter memories of Texas land, weather, food and democracy, British capital helped to restore the war-ravaged Texas economy by buying and leasing vast acreage at inflated prices, hiring Texas "cattle bosses" for thousands of dollars a year and Texas cowboys for the princely sum of $25 to $30 a month, paying such taxes as they could not avoid, and supplementing the income of "some state officials and more lobbyists."[102]

The British introduced barbed-wire and electric fences, steel windmills, deep wells, dipping vats and, for better or worse, Johnson grass to northwest Texas. They also experimented with various crops and finally, in an attempt to unload their vast Panhandle acreage, made great efforts to bring settlers to northwest Texas. Most important to the future of the Texas cattle industry, perhaps, was the British involvement in introducing improved stock to the western range.[103]

For hundreds of years English breeders had experimented with new strains of cattle on the British Isles with the intention of maximizing the amount of beef per individual animal. Early in the 19th century purebred Hereford and Shorthorn stock were imported for the first time to North America, and by 1879 purebred Herefords reached the Panhandle. Just at the time, therefore, when English corporations began to make heavy investments in Texas cattle ranches, the Longhorns were first crossbred with meatier but less range-toughened stock.[104]

Longhorns and Herefords on the Texas Panhandle, 1908

Because the Longhorns brought a much lower price on the Chicago market than did steers of improved breeds from the Midwest, English ranch managers imported thousands of purebred bulls to Texas during the 1880's. Shorthorn, Hereford, Scotch polled and Galloway bulls were crossed with the best-looking Longhorn cows and heifers. Breeders soon found that for the first cross with the Longhorn, nothing was superior to the Shorthorn. By continually using Shorthorns, however, the breed soon lost the hardihood necessary for life on the plains. Herefords, on the other hand, were found to produce calves nearly as sturdy as their native forebears while carrying nearly twice the beef. As one English ranch manager observed, "I do not suppose any cross will produce an animal so well suited to the range as the original long-horned Texan, but you can improve the appearance and weight of Texas cattle so much by crossing with well-bred bulls that it pays handsomely to do so, so long as you can avoid rendering the herd too tender."[105]

By the dawning of the 20th century the names of a few dust-blown cow towns—Tennyson, Wellington, Clarendon, Salisbury, Stratford, Hereford—seemed the only reminder of the former English presence, the last and only memorial. Nevertheless, English blood, English labor, English money and English technology made a tremendous contribution to the opening of the Panhandle. Without these gifts the rangeland of northwest Texas would have been a generation later in its development.

"The English get homesick because they cannot get gooseberries and 'arf-and-'arf and Lea & Perrin's sauce, growing on every mesquite-tree in Texas. They forget to give any credit to the watermelons, the figs, and other good things that they get in Texas, and that they could not raise, even in a hothouse, in England.

The English immigrant misses the shady lanes, the ivy-clad ruins, and the spires of the village church peeping through the trees: he experiences considerable difficulty in finding these things on the prairie near New Philadelphia. He misses all of them very much, but he is not as liable to miss his meals as he would be in England. There is at New Philadelphia no shady lane with violets nestling under the hedgerows, and there is also no landlord there for him to call master: so it is no wonder he feels a little homesick."

Alex E. Sweet and J. Armoy Knox, *On a Mexican Mustang through Texas* (London: Chatto and Windus, 1905), page 198.

Chapter 5
Civilizing
the Wild Frontier

Although he brought an undeniable touch of class to cow towns of the Texas Panhandle, the English cowboy never considered himself a deliberately refining factor in the Lone Star State. To the romantic English adventurer, centuries removed as he was from a wilderness experience and nurtured on the popular novels of the charm of a rugged, rustic existence far from cities and civilization, the West was a place of beauty, novelty and challenge to be tasted, enjoyed and left unspoiled.

Even to the English capitalist who viewed the West strictly as an area for financial exploitation, the American version of progress was undesirable. His investments in the range cattle industry gave him no direct stake in seeing the region fill with farms and cities as in the East; rather, he preferred that it remain an unstructured wilderness.[1]

Other Englishmen, however, came to Texas with a view to establishing homes for their families, and to these men and women the establishment of law and order, education, transportation, and the arts and letters were vastly important. Scarcely has any other immigrant group of the same size provided so many remarkable contributors to these goals.

Perhaps better than any other, the sons and daughters of Captain J. Bertie Cator exemplify the commitment to the development of Texas by an English family. Descended from a long line of seamen, Captain Cator resolved that his sons would break with family tradition. He would not have them "sacrificed to a life of hardship." Instead, in 1871, he sent the eldest two to Texas.

Having but a small patrimony with which to establish themselves, James and Arthur (Bob) Cator began their American careers as buffalo hunters. They first followed the Kansas herd to the vicinity of Ft. Hays, where they lost a yoke of oxen and a saddle horse to a November blizzard. Nevertheless, they were able to recoup their losses by the sale of 300 hides and set out after the diminishing herds toward the Texas Panhandle. There they prospered for three years before losing six mules, four horses, three wagons, a tent, a large stock of provisions and hunting supplies, and 898 buffalo hides to the Comanches at the Second Battle of Adobe Walls in 1874. With typical British understatement the brothers reported that "they felt their parents did not understand the situations they would face in America."

Before long, with the buffalo diminished to near-extinction, Jim and Bob established a trading post, Zulu Stockade, at the site of their hunting camp. Zulu was the main trading post for the country north of the Canadian River for at least ten years and was a federal post office

Palo Duro Canyon

from 1878 to 1912. The Cators bought their first cattle in 1878, and Jim acquired land along Palo Duro Creek in 1879.

In the fall of 1879 Clara Cator arrived in Hansford County accompanied by her brother Bert and a Miss Ludlow (who soon married Bob Cator). The two women were apparently the first white women to settle in the area north of the Canadian. Clara was an adventurous, fun-loving girl, well endowed with common sense. She kept house for her brothers until her marriage to Tascosa schoolteacher Clayton McCrea. Bert became a cowhand, breaker of wild horses, and later, farmer and rancher.

On a trip to England in late 1879 Jim became engaged to Edith Land, daughter of a well-to-do physician. He planned to return for her in 1883. In the interim he built a rock house on Palo Duro Creek, now the oldest building in Hansford County, completed in 1882. Just as

Original rock house built by James H. Cator

Jim was preparing to return to England for his bride, the terrible blizzard of 1882 struck, wiping out nearly all the stock in the area. It took Jim and Bob five years to recover their losses, but finally in May 1887 Edith, accompanied by her brother, Arthur Land, met and married Jim in Dodge City, Kansas.

The fourth Cator brother, Leslie, came to Dodge City in 1882 with his wife and son, who, however, soon returned to England. Leslie endured some ridicule from the local cowboys because of his spiffy derby, spats and tight pants. A blacksmith by trade, however, he was quite capable of defending his honor, and the taunting ceased when he soundly thrashed his worst tormentor. Leslie joined his brothers and sister in Hansford County in the early 1890's.

Also in the 1880's Bob moved to Oregon, but Jim continued to make significant contributions to Hansford County. In addition to being a major force in bringing county status to the region, he served as sheriff, judge and treasurer as well as president of Hansford's first bank. He was a pioneer in selective breeding in the area and introduced both wheat and alfalfa to the Panhandle.

Brother Bert followed in his footsteps to serve several terms as sheriff, and Leslie spent many years as Hansford's judge and tax assessor. Citizens of the county characterized the Cators as "sturdy English men . . . neighbors and friends, staunch and true . . . indomitable and necessary people to the taming and future development of the great way" on the Texas Panhandle.[2]

Left to right: James H. Cator, unidentified woman and child, Edith Cator, Mrs. Bert Cator, Bert Cator, Louie Cator Nobles, Gid Nobles and James F. Cator

Before anyone could succeed at farming or ranching in Texas, however, the problem of depredations by Comanche, Apache and other warlike Indian raiders had to be alleviated. In this epic struggle, too, the English played their role. Not only did native English comprise a large segment of the regular United States Army establishment on the Texas frontier,[3] many others served as volunteers or as Texas Rangers against the hostile tribes.

Frank Collinson, for example, a cowboy and buffalo hunter in Texas since leaving his native Yorkshire in 1872, participated in the battle of Yellow House Draw in 1877, one of the last fights between Anglo-Americans and Comanches fought on the Llano Estacado. Although confined by treaty to reservations in present-day Oklahoma, many young Indian warriors, longing for the freer lives of their ancestors, raided the cattle ranches and buffalo hunters' camps of the Panhandle.

Frank Collinson

Collinson, who had lost heavily to the marauding bands, joined a group of buffalo hunters bent upon revenge. "The spring weather was fine for an outing," he recalled, "and I rode my good horse over virgin territory, glad I was alive and looking forward to a scalp hunt." In his youthful dreams of glory he even saw himself sending one of the grisly trophies to his family in England "to give them an idea of the wild and wooly West in far-off Texas."

The band of buffalo hunters located the Comanche camp and began a premature celebration of an anticipated victory around a whiskey barrel. By morning the whiskey was gone, and each hunter was boasting of the scalps of Indians he had not yet seen. As the men mounted and headed toward the enemy encampment, Collinson observed, "many of them were still half-Shot." The buffalo hunters attacked the village at a gallop. The element of surprise had been lost, however, and the charging hunters were subjected to galling fire. Although they overran the village, their casualties were heavy. Sober and properly led, the hunters "could have whipped half the Comanche tribe," but, half drunk, overconfident and totally undisciplined, they "got licked and well licked."

Disgusted by this slipshod operation, Collinson rode into Fort Griffin and signed on as a scout for the Tenth Cavalry. Within months, however, the Indian threat to west Texas had been crushed, and the English cowboy drifted out to New Mexico where he rode for cattle king John Chisum and fought in the Lincoln County war alongside Billy the Kid.

Eventually he returned to Texas, where, after years of roaming from ranch to ranch, he bought a spread of his own and settled down with his Scottish-born bride. After retiring from ranch life in 1922, he published in *Ranch Romances* numerous exciting and authentic short stories based on his life in the saddle. Frank Collinson died in El Paso in 1943 at the age of 87.[4]

Besides such rough-and-ready volunteers as Collinson, England provided professional law enforcement officers for the unruly Texas frontier. Among the many English-born Texas Rangers was William L. Rudd. Like Frank Collinson, Rudd was a Yorkshireman who immigrated to Texas in 1872, where he eventually enlisted under the command of the famed Ranger Captain L.H. McNelly in the Special State Troop of the Frontier Battalion.

In a 14-year career with the Rangers Rudd fought Mexican cattle thieves on both sides of the Rio Grande, pursued Texas outlaws Sam Bass, John Wesley Hardin and King Fisher, and reestablished peace in DeWitt County in the wake of the notorious Sutton-Taylor feud. Along the way he earned the rank of corporal, then first lieutenant and finally captain of his troop, as well as the colorful nickname, "Colorado Chico."

His men characterized him as "a little bit of a red-headed, red-faced Englishman who always rode the biggest horse in the troop," and who, although a serious officer, was also fun loving. Highly sociable, after leaving the Rangers in 1884, Captain Rudd rounded out his career in law enforcement as sheriff of Karnes County.[5]

Not all of Britannia's sons remained law-abiding once they left the strictures of civilization for the freedom of the frontier. One such was Ben Thompson, born in 1843 in Yorkshire, whose family moved to Austin in 1845. Thompson was paid the highest compliment of perhaps any member of his "trade" by the renowned Bat Masterson, former marshal of Dodge City, Kansas. He was, according to Masterson, the greatest gunfighter of all. "Others missed at times, but Ben Thompson was as delicate and certain in action as a Swiss watch." Thirty-two men fell before Thompson's gun, all, Masterson claimed, "killed openly and manly."

The consummate dandy, Thompson was famous for his silk hats, tailored suits and waxed mustache as well as for his lethal aim.

Ben Thompson

As owner of the faro concession at Austin's Iron Front Saloon, he made a small fortune and enhanced his already legendary reputation as a fast gun. Thus, when Austin needed a new marshal in 1880, Thompson was elected to the post. The Texas capital was soon so free of outlaws that its chief law enforcement officer grew bored. Marshal Thompson, it is reported, began drinking heavily and took delight in shooting out Austin's street lights and the hats from the heads of salesmen from the East. In 1882 he gunned down a personal enemy in a San Antonio shoot-out and was involved for months in legal proceedings. He resigned his office at this time, although he eventually was acquitted and returned in triumph to Austin.

Thompson met his own demise in 1884, killed beside the equally notorious King Fisher in a box in San Antonio's Vaudeville Theatre. The most famous of English gunslingers was buried beneath a marble monument which he had won at faro during his glory days at the old Iron Front Saloon.[6]

San Antonio's "Fatal Corner," 1884

As well as enforcing (and occasionally breaking) the law on the frontier and on the city streets, English-born Texans did considerable service in organizing and filling the ranks of the state's judicial system.

Although liberally spiced with Spanish legal practices, Texas jurisprudence was most heavily influenced by that of England. Quite naturally, therefore, men such as Henry Marcus Holmes would rise to the top of the legal profession in their adopted land. Born in Bristol in 1836, Holmes moved with his family in 1850 to the frontier community of Waco. At age 15 he joined the United States Army and served in Texas with the 2nd Dragoons. Holmes rose through the ranks to the grade of major of the 24th Infantry, a regiment of all black enlisted men serving under white officers, which compiled an outstanding record against Comanche and Apache raiders in west Texas.

In 1871 Major Holmes mustered out of the army at Fort McKavett and began the practice of law in Mason and Menard counties. "Affable and obliging in his manners and having keen blue eyes and physical development according to the best classes of the English type," he was soon elected justice of the peace and then rose through the judicial ranks as quickly as he had the military. Holmes served as county attorney during the infamous "Hoodoo War," a feud between factions of the Anglo and German-Texan segments of Mason County's population in 1875. He later became a county judge and assistant attorney general under the John Ireland administration where he was charac-

Henry Marcus Holmes

terized as "indefatigable at his desk and of immeasurable benefit to his office through his appearance in court."

The crowning of Henry Holmes's career came with the election of his first American friend, Lawrence Sullivan Ross, as governor of Texas. Holmes was appointed "personal and confidential secretary" to Ross, a position from which he wielded considerable power for public land management and railroad regulation. Returning to Mason County with the end of the Ross administration, Holmes was instrumental in the founding of the Texas State Bar Association, an organization which he served until his death in 1895.[7]

While these Englishmen, and hundreds more besides, pushed back the frontier, building farms and ranches and helping to create the legend of the Old West, others came behind to bring the amenities of civilization to the raw new country.

James E. Thompson of Northwich, for example, received medical training at the University of London and in Paris and Vienna. In 1891 he left a position as Resident Surgeon of the Manchester Royal Infirmary to accept the Chair of Surgery in the newly organized medical department at The University of Texas.

James E. Thompson

Dr. Thompson claimed to "have been endowed with the spirit of a pioneer" to have left his well-established family and career in

England to accept a position in a newly founded and as yet unorganized medical school "in the uncivilized part of the world called Texas." In Galveston he found a fledgling institution "starved physically by want of equipment and mentally by want of a library, cut off from the educational influences of the learned society by our geographical position." His talent, courage and devotion slowly turned it into one of the foremost medical schools in the country.

Always somewhat reserved, extremely articulate, and neatly and tastefully attired, Dr. Thompson remained an enigma to many of his students and colleagues, and they to him. Wishing to give his sons the advantages of both the old world and the new, he took them each summer to England, and all four attended both the British-type Upper Canada College in Toronto and The University of Texas.

The want of equipment and library facilities in Texas were not alone in dismaying this man whom William Mayo called "the Dean of Texas Surgeons." On one occasion a resentful colleague attacked him at a Galveston County Medical Society meeting with a loaded gun. Dr. Thompson overpowered his adversary and removed his weapon, a skill seldom practiced at the Manchester Royal Infirmary.

Adding insult to injury, in 1917 Governor James E. "Pa" Ferguson demanded Dr. Thompson's resignation from the medical branch faculty on the grounds that he was not an American citizen. Ferguson's impeachment obviated this shameful situation, but, nevertheless, Dr. Thompson, who had served in the U.S. Army Medical Corps in 1912, became a naturalized United States citizen in June 19, 1917.[8]

For 36 years Dr. Thompson was perhaps the prime mover in the establishment of medical education in Texas. His vast contributions as teacher and organizer to the learning and practice of medicine were felt not only in Texas but throughout the United States. This eminent physician was a member of almost every learned and professional society in his field, both in America and Great Britain. He served as president of the Southern Surgical Association, first vice-president of the American Surgical Association, first president of the Texas Surgical Society, and vice-president of the Texas State Medical Association. In addition, Dr. Thompson was a prolific author, publishing a great many influential articles in medical journals both in the United States and in Europe.[9]

Among the Englishmen who made major contributions to the causes of religion and social reform in Texas was London-born Hudson Stuck. As an 1885 graduate of King's College, Stuck tossed a coin—

heads for Australia, tails for Texas. It landed tails, and the young man soon found himself punching cattle near Junction City and teaching in one-room schools at Copperas Creek, San Angelo and San Marcos. In 1889, however, he entered the Theological Department of the University of the South, Sewanee, Tennessee, and was ordained as an Episcopal priest in 1892. For the next two years he served as rector of Grace Church, Cuero, before moving to St. Matthew's Cathedral in Dallas, where in 1896 he became dean.

Casting himself as "the social conscience of north Texas," Stuck preached and practiced a "muscular Christianity" which demanded that individuals be their brother's keeper. His sermons condemned lynching, championed gun control and demanded recreational areas for the city's poor. Among his accomplishments away from the pulpit were a night school for millworkers, a home for indigent women and St. Matthew's Children's Home. Stuck coauthored and helped to shepherd through the legislature the first state law condemning the "indefensible abuse" of child labor in Texas.

Finding himself too "comfortable and happy" in Dallas, Stuck sought new challenges in 1904, moving to Alaska there to "suffer hardship for the Kingdom." As Archdeacon of the Yukon he administered 250,000 square miles by boat and dogsled and, in 1913, organized and led the first party to climb Mt. McKinley. The author of five books and scores of journal articles, Stuck died at Fort Yukon in 1920.[10]

In the fields of civil engineering and architecture British Texans also made great contributions. Perhaps the most notable name in Texas's transportation history is that of the Welsh railroad builder, "Colonel" Morgan Jones. Born at Tregynon, Montgomery County, Wales, in 1839, Jones succumbed to the lure of the rising industrial order early in his life. Fascinated by the steam engine, he left the family farm, "Vachwen," at age 19 to work on the Welsh railroads. By this time, however, Great Britain was completely criss-crossed with rail links, and the young man needed new spaces to absorb his energies.

Those spaces were fortuitously provided in 1865 when the United States Congress chartered a transcontinental railroad to be built west from Omaha, Nebraska. Morgan Jones came to America in 1869 as a representative of a British explosives company, with a shipload of dynamite consigned to the Union Pacific Railroad. More fortunate than most European immigrants of this period, he arrived with sufficient resources to supply his personal needs for some months, as well as seven

Morgan Jones, 1880

years of experience in railroad building, a highly marketable skill in midcentury America.

He became friends with General Grenville Dodge, Chief Engineer for Construction for Union Pacific, and, after three years of apprentice work for the railroad, was promoted to the position of construction supervisor for the Texas and Pacific Railroad's proposed line from Texarkana to Fort Worth. Bringing this project to completion on time against severe handicaps, he won the further admiration of General Dodge, the West's greatest builder of railroads. Dodge hired Jones to push the line on from Fort Worth to Denver, a 20-year undertaking for which he was rewarded with the presidency of the Fort Worth and Denver City Railway.

Establishing his headquarters at Abilene, Jones extended the Wichita Valley Railroad north to Wichita Falls and the Abilene Southern, which he personally owned, south to Ballinger. In total, Morgan Jones supervised the construction of more than 1,000 miles of track in Texas.

A tireless worker, Jones designed and developed the first pipeline to bring fresh water to Galveston Island, while he was ostensibly vaca-

Morgan Jones in conductor's uniform, c. 1900

Morgan Jones in Fort Worth & Denver City Railway office, c. 1895

tioning there. Expanding into banking, mining, ranching, real estate, oil and cotton interests, "Colonel" Jones became fabulously wealthy, yet always carried his lunch in a brown paper bag. As a result of this Welsh immigrant's energy, skill and foresight, the cities of Abilene, Wichita Falls, Fort Worth, Amarillo, Clarendon, Seymour and scores of smaller communities blossomed from the railroad's steel vine. Jones's efforts linked to eastern markets and cultural centers the millions of acres claimed by farmers and ranchers, and ensured the coming of civilization to the west Texas rangelands.[11]

One of the finest of Texas's 19th century architects was also English born and educated. Alfred Giles, a graduate of London's King's College, came to San Antonio in 1875 at age 22, seeking a dry climate

Alfred Giles, c. 1875

in which to recuperate from rheumatic fever. Here he established himself as an architect, and in a career which spanned 44 years he constructed more than $20,000,000 worth of buildings in Texas and northern Mexico. His designs include the Edward Steves and Carl Groos residences in the King William Historic District of San Antonio, the old Gillespie County Courthouse in Fredericksburg, the old Bandera County Jail in Bandera, the Wilson County Courthouse in Floresville, and the Webb County Courthouse in Laredo. Giles's firm reroofed the Alamo mission chapel and in 1912 submitted a design for a monument

Gillespie County Courthouse, 1911

to be constructed in Alamo Plaza, to honor the heroes of the Texas Revolution. This monument was to be 802 feet high, 250 feet taller than the Washington Monument and, in fact, the tallest tower in the world. Although the Alamo monument was never erected, Giles's other structures are still among Texas's proudest landmarks, studied by students of architecture to this day.[12]

In addition to being Texas's most celebrated architect, Giles was also a successful rancher, owning and managing, in partnership with his brother-in-law, Judge John Herndon James, 13,000 acres near the village of Comfort 50 miles northwest of San Antonio. Here he raised horses, mules, registered Aberdeen Angus cattle and Angora goats. Hillingdon, the Giles ranch, was, according to novelist Richard Harding Davis, "the exception in the rule of failures of our English cousins. . . . Hillingdon looks in summer, when the imported Scotch cattle are grazing over it, like a bit out of the Lake Country."[13]

Quite possibly Giles's intention at Hillingdon was to transform "some corner of a foreign field" into a reminder of his home country. He and his wife, the Texas-born daughter of an English father, did leave Texas at one time, planning to establish a permanent home in London.

Once there, however, they grew to miss the people and countryside of Texas and so soon returned to their Hill Country ranch. Unlike the English cowboys and capitalists of the west Texas frontier, Englishmen such as Giles were beginning to consider themselves Texans and not tourists or temporary residents.

"Hillingdon," 1895

More than any other immigrant group, save only the Germans, the English are responsible in Texas for the perpetuation of a regard for the arts and letters, the crowning achievement of any civilization. Even before the trans-Pecos frontier was free of serious outlaw depredations, English actors and musicians were endeavoring to bring a bit of culture to west Texas by means of traveling theatrical and musical events. Certainly the most famous of English entertainers, if not the most respectable, was the "Jersey Lily," Miss Lillie Langtry.

Miss Langtry, on her first Texas tour, was received with adulation by the cowboys and the inhabitants of the dusty western villages. When, on one occasion, her railroad car jolted from the rails, the local citizens staged for her entertainment an impromptu rodeo. "Among other items," she recalls in her memoirs, "a raw broncho was lassoed, and a substantial present was to be bestowed by me on whoever should succeed in mounting and riding it up to the inverted barrel on which

Lillie Langtry

I was placed." Only after a score of aspirants, including one actor from her own troupe, were unhorsed and badly bruised did the beast submit "to a seasoned *vaquero*."

A greater surprise yet was bestowed upon her some years later when the redoubtable Judge Roy Bean, "The Law West of the Pecos," named a town in her honor. The "embryo city," a stop on the Southern Pacific railroad, invited her to visit, but, being at the time otherwise engaged, she offered the city instead an ornamental drinking fountain. Judge Bean, her great admirer, quickly replied that "it would be quite useless, as the only thing the citizens of Langtry did *not* drink was water."

Only after the death of Judge Bean did Miss Langtry have occasion to visit her namesake. As her train crossed the Pecos and drew nearer and nearer to "her" town, her excitement grew. Although the "sun was blazing down on the parched sandy plain, with its monotonous clothing of sagebrush and low growing cactus," she sat "agog" in anticipation of the charms of Langtry.

When her train came to a sudden halt, a glance from her window "revealed no reason why we should pause there rather than at any other point of the continuous grey desert." She was in fact in Langtry, but because her car was the last of the train, she could see no sign of human habitation.

Nevertheless, she was enthusiastically but respectfully greeted by the village justice of the peace, the postmaster, the station master "and other persons of consequence" in Langtry, plus a number of cowboys "in their finest leathers and most flamboyant shirts, as became the occasion." In addition to having the town named for her, Miss Langtry learned that Judge Bean's saloon was called the "Jersey Lilly" and that his pet monkey was likewise "The Lily."

Judge Roy Bean and the Jersey Lilly, c. 1896

During a reception in the Judge's saloon, Miss Langtry was regaled with Roy Bean tales and presented with his hand-engraved revolver, which she later hung "in a place of honor" in her English home, and his favorite pet, a large cinnamon bear whose name is unknown. Very likely it was Lily as well.[14]

A British contributor to American journalism was Devonport native Joseph Lancaster who survived the battles of Goliad and San Jacinto to return to Alabama and Mississippi where his newspapers served as a forum of pro-Texas annexation sentiment. With Texas's admission to the Union, Lancaster returned to Washington-on-the-Brazos to establish the *Texas Ranger*, one of the most influential newspapers in antebellum Texas. Although Lancaster and his two sons served the Confederacy for four years as soldiers, the *Ranger* did not miss an issue. Eva Lancaster, his wife, managed and edited the paper throughout the war.

At the war's end the Lancasters moved their paper to Austin where Joseph became head of the State Library, a position which he held from 1872 until his death in 1874.[15]

Other and lasting contributions to Texas were made by a number of English editors and publishers. Manxman David Richardson, for example, who came to Texas in 1852 at the age of 37, is credited with establishing the *Texas Almanac*, the oldest continuously operating business institution in Texas and a major force in the development of the state. The *Almanac* grew out of the *Galveston News*, first printed on a hand press in a one-room shack on Galveston Island in April 1842. In an effort to attract settlers to the state, Richardson, with some colleagues from the *News*, published the first *Almanac* in 1857. This annual was largely responsible for the funding of railroads linking the Texas interior with the state's ports, and by the time of the Civil War the *Galveston News* had become the most influential newspaper in the southwestern United States.

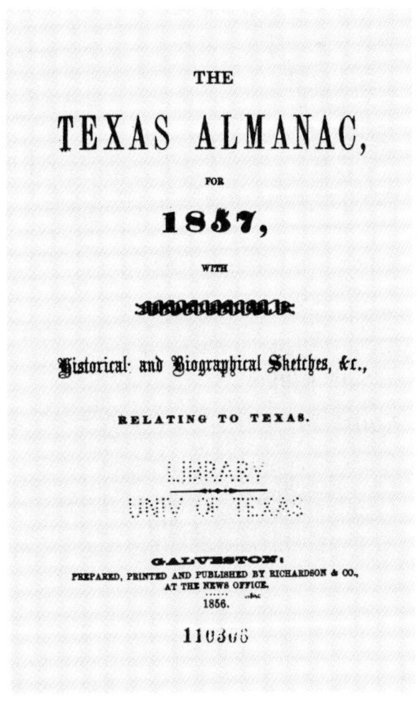

The shortages created by Union blockade and temporary occupation of Galveston caused Richardson to transfer his publishing operation to Austin in 1863. There he printed the *State Gazette* on newsprint made of corn shucks and on wallpaper stripped from walls. Richardson returned to the *Almanac* in 1867 and served as its national advertising agent until his death in 1871.

A second English newspaperman who began his career with the *Galveston News* and the *Texas Almanac* was George Bannerman Dealey, "the Dean of American journalists." The Dealey family immigrated in 1870 from Manchester to Galveston, where young George became an office boy for the *News* at $3.00 a week. Within 15 years he had worked himself up within the organization to the point of founding and serving as first manager of the Dallas *Morning News*, a satellite of the Galveston paper. The *Morning News* proved tremendously influential in building Dallas, then a north Texas town "beginning to put on the airs of a city." According to one admirer, "the Dallas of today is [Dealey's] monument as St. Paul's of London immortalizes the name of Sir Christopher Wren." In 1921 Dealey became president of the paper that he founded, and his family still owns considerable radio, television and publishing affiliates in the city that he helped to build.[16]

George B. Dealey   James Q. Dealey

A younger brother of George B. Dealey also carved a distinguished career in the realm of Texas letters. Beginning, as had his older brother, with the *Galveston News*, James Quayle Dealey graduated from Brown University in 1890 and became a member of the faculty of Denton State Normal, now North Texas State University. In 1895 he completed his Ph.D. at Brown, where he remained to teach political and social science. Dealey became one of America's pioneer sociologists, lecturing widely and accumulating an impressive bibliography of scholarly publication until he returned to Texas in 1929 to become editor of his brother's famous newspaper.[17]

Yet another Englishman, Henry Hutchings of Somersetshire, was founder and publisher of the Austin *Evening News* and the influential Austin *Statesman*. From 1911 Hutchings served as Texas's adjutant general, and with the United States' entry into World War I he organized and led the 71st Infantry Brigade. Hutchings served as secretary of state under Governor Pat Neff and later returned to his old post as adjutant general until 1935.[18]

A host of other English-born Texans made major if less spectacular contributions to the development of Texas. Frank Desprez was born in London in 1853 and apprenticed by his father to the copperplate engraving trade. The lure of "the open air and open sky/In Texas, down by the Rio Grande" overwhelmed him, however, and at age 21 he left England for the United States where, for about three years, he was "occupied on a cattle ranch." Although brief, his sojourn in Texas left a lasting impression upon his imagination. Desprez, after his return to England, became drama critic and editor of *The Era*, "the supreme authority on matters theatrical" in London, and writer of some modestly successful operettas.[19] Ten years after leaving Texas, however, this gentleman with waxed mustache and monocle wrote a poem of his adventures which J. Frank Dobie remembered as being regularly "recited on Friday afternoons in country schoolhouses from Montana to the Gulf of Mexico."[20]

In the mood of Kipling's soldier-heroes, back in England but pining for "someplace east of Suez," Desprez remembers Texas fondly:

> It's all very well to write reviews,
> And carry umbrellas, and keep dry shoes,
> * * *
> But tonight I'm sick of the whole affair,
> I want free life, and I want fresh air;
> And I sigh for the canter after the cattle
> The crack of the whips like shots in a battle.

Although considered somewhat risqué by the more refined, "Lasca" captured the popular imagination of Texas as no poem has before or since. Dobie testified that "many a lad who had never read a poem knew ["Lasca"] by heart," and Texas ballad collector John A. Lomax learned the poem during his first year in school and recited it, in 1911, to the convention of the Modern Language Association.[21] Several dramatic readings of "Lasca" were recorded for Thomas Edison's newest invention, the phonograph, and it was set to music and was sung for years in Europe and America. A silent film version featured a "stampede" in which the cattle never moved faster than a trot "in spite of every inducement from behind."

Desprez died in London in 1916, well regarded personally and professionally by all who knew him. His successful years as critic and dramatist were in his own mind eclipsed, however, by the brief three spent as a cowboy.

> . . . I do not care
> For things that are, like the things that were.
> Does half my heart lie buried there
> In Texas, down by the Rio Grande?[22]

William J. Marsh, for 50 years choirmaster and organist at St. Patrick's Cathedral in Fort Worth, wrote the music and, with Mrs. Gladys Yokum Wright, coauthored the lyrics to "Texas, Our Texas," the

William J. Marsh, 1929

official state song.[23] Charles N. Fisher of London was among the pioneers in the important east Texas lumber industry.[24] Edmond E. Risien from Dover is known as "the Father of the Texas pecan industry."[25]

According to one story, perhaps apocryphal, an Englishman even invented Texas chili. Having settled in San Antonio in the 1880's, this unnamed gentleman blended locally available chili peppers and oregano as a substitute for the curry for which he had developed a taste while tiger hunting in India.[26]

As Texas grew and prospered she began to repay her debt to "the grandmother country." During the First World War many English Texans returned to Europe to help defend England under the Union Jack and the Stars and Stripes. Godfrey John Boyle, the eighth viscount Chetwynd, was among the scores of young aristocratic Englishmen to come

Godfrey John Boyle,
eighth viscount Chetwynd

to Texas as cattle and sheep ranchers in the 1870's. Cowboy, camp cook and deputy sheriff of Tom Green County as a young man, Chetwynd returned to England to head the great Vickers Steel Mill during World War I. Strangled by the German submarine blockade, England was suffering a critical munitions shortage when Chetwynd implemented numerous radical innovations in the manufacture of shells. Under his direction 10,000 workers brought production up to demand and saved the British Expeditionary Force in France. Following England's crisis, however, Viscount Chetwynd returned to Texas to live out his years as rancher and prospector near San Angelo.[27]

Texas also helped to train aviators for Great Britain's Royal Flying Corps. San Antonio's Kelly Air Force Base, in fact, is named for Lieutenant George Kelly, a London-born pilot who was killed in an airplane crash at Fort Sam Houston on May 10, 1911. When Kelly's defective aircraft stalled over an infantry encampment, the flyer banked his plane sharply to the left, ensuring both the survival of the troops below and his own death in the inevitable crash.[28]

Lt. George Edward Maurice Kelly, 1911

Kelly Field, San Antonio, c. 1925

The greatest single influx of British immigrants to Texas in the 20th century followed World War II when a large number of wartime brides accompanied their soldier husbands back to Texas. These women comprise a large segment of the 16,123 persons of English and 440 of Welsh birth who, according to the 1980 United States census, make their homes in Texas.[29] This figure, small by most standards of comparison, fails to reflect the tremendous historical impact of Great Britain and the immigration of English people upon the growth and development of Texas or the mutual love and respect between these two English-speaking peoples.

British novelist Graham Greene announced on August 23, 1953, from London the formation of the Anglo-Texan Society which he would serve as first president. Growing from numerous personal friendships and the mutual admiration between Englishmen and Texans, the society defined as its general objective the establishment of closer social and cultural ties between England and Texas, "which occupies a special historical position not only in relation to the United States but also in relation to Great Britain." Asked if he agreed with the allegation often made by other Americans that Texans boast about their state, Greene replied, "No, I think they just tell the truth."[30]

Greene and his associates hoped to establish "special premises" in London for welcoming visitors from Texas, where they might be provided "with a hospitality equal to that which Texas has traditionally given to English visitors." Although such a permanent establishment has so far failed to materialize, another prominent member of the Anglo-Texan Society, Alfred Lord Bossom, architect of Dallas's Magnolia Building, took delight in entertaining Texan visitors at the House of Lords, an honor seldom bestowed upon the common tourist.

With Bossom's death in 1965, Ted Jones, a London public relations agent, became president of the society. "I want Britain to remember always its ties to Texas," Jones says. "And I hope Texans will always have a bit of a British accent."[31]

The spirit of the extraordinary relationship between England and Texas was admirably phrased by the Texas-born president of the United States, Lyndon B. Johnson. "I take special pride," he declared, "in the long history of cordial relations between Texas, as a Republic and as a state, with England. Oceans separate us. Purpose unites us. We, in the United States, recognize that our sanctuary is not the sea between us but the spirit among us."[32]

Between 1842 and 1845 Ashbel Smith served as the Republic of Texas's Minister to the Court of St. James. The Texas Legation was located in premises owned by a firm of wine merchants which had been established in the 17th century (and today still owns and operates from the same premises). A plaque by the door reads:

The Welsh in Texas

Although in a great many respects they were very much the same as other British, the Welsh of the island's mountainous west country have historically harbored distinct cultural characteristics which effectively separated them from their English neighbors. Predominantly a mining people and speaking a language "as sweet as ditties highly penn'd/sung by a fair queen in a summer's bower," the Welsh in Texas proved far less assimilable than the English or Scots. Intensely clannish, generally technologically less advanced than the English and relatively isolated in their mountain valleys, the Welsh were content to remain farmers and coal miners generation after generation. With a precipitous drop in wages paid to miners in the 1870's, however, thousands were forced to look away from their ancestral homeland to a new start beyond the Atlantic. The very remoteness and loneliness of the Texas frontier, an aspect of existence which frightened many would-be pioneers from the developing region,

Welsh miners leaving Merthyr Tydvil, 1873

encouraged the Welsh to hope that here was a place where they might maintain their way of life and language.[1]

Severe depression, especially in the iron industry, beginning in 1876, left two million miners unemployed, and many of these Welshmen were struck by "Texas fever." For the remainder of the decade Welsh newspapers gave considerable coverage to the merits of Texas as a potential area of settlement for laid-off miners, and in 1878 a Texas emigration society was formed in the Rhondda Valley. Planners envisioned a community of Welsh agrarians in west Texas, providing homes and employment for the immigrants and raising wages of the Welsh at home by reducing somewhat the labor force at the coal pits. Large-scale emigration would be the safety valve which would redress the imbalances between too many miners and too little demand for coal.

Members of the emigration society agreed to contribute initially £5 each plus two shillings and sixpence per month until enough money had been accumulated to send six to eight families to Texas. In addition to their passage, each family would receive 80 acres of land, a house, a yoke of oxen, two cows, a dozen chickens, two pigs, a set of farming implements, cooking utensils, a stove and £10 per month for groceries until their first crop should come in. The society's leadership was convinced that, with such liberal terms, they would have 100,000 members within a few months and that, in less than five years, the society would be sending out more than a thousand people a month.

In August the Merthyr *Telegraph* reported the departure of a large number of emigrants from the Rhymney and Rhondda valleys under the auspices of the Workmen's Emigration Society. These hopeful new settlers landed in Galveston in November and from there took trains to their New Philadelphia colony in Wharton County. There they found houses and stock ready as promised and food available on company credit. This promising start, however, was cruelly deceptive.[2]

"They were not ready for us," one immigrant wrote to friends in Wales. Although the houses had been built and were "quite as good as I had expected," stoves had not yet been ordered from New York. By January 1880 credit for food was cut off because funds from the society were not forthcoming. Although the Welsh settlers were very well pleased with their new homes and surroundings, and found the "Texicans" to be "more intelligent men than those of the coal mines" and "gentlemen in every sense of the word," they had arrived too late in the year to plant, and without credit at the grocers' they were forced to move on.

Hearing of wages to be had mining coal in the Indian Territory, most of the infant colony drifted north out of Texas. "Turning my back on the place," one recorded, was "the most heartbreaking thing I ever had to do."[3]

As word of the New Philadelphia failure filtered back to Wales, Texas emigration came to an abrupt halt.[4] Although the efforts of the Workmen's Emigration Society had come at last to naught, and although Welsh settlement in Texas has remained sparse, Welsh impact upon Texas has not been inconsiderable. From the native Welsh who died in defense of the Alamo to Morgan Jones who built west Texas's railway system, the Welsh Texans have been a brave and enterprising addition to the republic's and state's rich cultural blend.

Notes

"Ingram's Walk"

1 Raymer Unwin, *The Defeat of John Hawkins: A Biography of His Third Slaving Voyage* (New York: Macmillan Company, 1960), pp. 189-211.

2 Sir John Hawkins, "A True Declaration of the Troublesome Voyage of M. John Hawkins," *Hakluyt's Voyages*, ed. Richard David (Boston: Houghton Mifflin Company, 1981), p. 404.

3 Ibid.

4 David Ingram, "The Relation of David Ingram of Barking, in the Countie of Essex, Sayler," *The Principall Navigations, Voiages and Discoveries of the English Nation*, ed. Richard Hakluyt (London: George Bishop, 1589; facsimile reprint, n.p.: Readex Microprint, 1966), pp. 557-58.

5 Ibid., p. 560.

6 Ibid., p. 559.

7 Carl A. Brasseaux and Richard E. Chandler, "The *Britain* Incident, 1769-1770: Anglo-Hispanic Tensions in the Western Gulf," *Southwestern Historical Quarterly* LXXXVII, 4 (April 1984): 357-58.

8 Isaac Joslin Cox, "The Louisiana-Texas Frontier," *The Quarterly of the Texas State Historical Association* X, 1 (July 1906): 36.

9 Ibid., p. 37.

10 Charlotte Erickson, "English," *The Harvard Encyclopedia of American Ethnic Groups*, ed. Stephen Thernstrom (Cambridge, Mass.: Harvard University Press, 1980), pp. 319-20.

Chapter 1

1 Amelia Williams, "A Critical Study of the Siege of the Alamo and of the Personnel of its Defenders," *Southwestern Historical Quarterly* XXXVII, 4 (April 1934): 242-89.

2 Marie Bennet Urwitz, "Valentine Bennet," *The Quarterly of the Texas State Historical Association* IX, 3 (January 1906): 145-56.

3 Walter Prescott Webb and H. Bailey Carroll, eds., *The Handbook of Texas*, 3 vols. (Austin: Texas State Historical Association, 1952, 1976), 2:595 ("Charles Shearn").

4 Ibid., p. 18 ("Joseph Lancaster"); Hobart Huson, "J. Lancaster, Pioneer Editor," Sinton *Enterprise*, October 1928.

5 Mrs. Dave Finkelstein, *John and Margaret Hallett, American Pioneers* (Hallettsville, Tex.: Hallettsville *Tribune*, 1951).

6 Webb and Carroll, 1:843 ("Thomas William House").

7 Lewis L. Gould, ed., "A Texan in London," *Southwestern Historical Quarterly* IXXIV, 4 (April 1981): 427-28, 433.

8 J.E. Erickson, "Origins of the Texas Bill of Rights," *Southwestern Historical Quarterly* LXII, 4 (April 1959): 457-66.

9 Hubert Howe Bancroft, *History of the North Mexican States and Texas, 1801-1889* (San Francisco: History Company, Publishers, 1889), p. 338.

10 William Kennedy, *Texas* (London: R. Hastings, 1841), I: vi.

11 David Urquhart, *Annexation of the Texas, A Case of War Between England and the United States* (London: James Maynard, 1844), pp. 23-24.

12 Clagette Blake, *Charles Elliot, R.N., 1801-1875* (London: Cleaver-Hume Press, 1960), p. 66.

13 N. Doran Maillard, *The History of the Republic of Texas* (London: Smith, Elder, and Company, 1842), p. ix.

14 Urquhart, pp. 17-18.

15 Maillard, p. xx.

16 Charles Sealsfield, *Frontierlife* (Philadelphia: Porter and Gates, 1852), pp. 171, 173-74; quoted in Ray Allen Billington, *Land of Savagery, Land of Promise* (New York: W.W. Norton and Company, 1981), p. 288.

17 George William Featherstonhaugh, *Excursions Through the Slave States* (London: J. Murray, 1844), II: 184.

18 Francis C. Sheridan, *Galveston Island*, ed. Willis W. Pratt (Austin: University of Texas Press, 1954), p. 119.

19 Ibid., p. 116.

20 Seymour V. Connor, *Adventure in Glory: The Saga of Texas, 1836-1849* (Austin: Steck-Vaughn, 1965), p. 57.

21 Ibid., pp. 58-59, 78-79.

22 Branch Tanner Archer, quoted in Kennedy, pp. v-vi.

23 Connor, p. 109; Bancroft, pp. 340-46.

24 Connor, p. 130.

25 Ibid., pp. 131-33, 138, 153, 160.

26 Blake, pp. xiv, 64, 69, 73.

27 Ibid., pp. 70, 71, 73.

28 Ibid., pp. 67, 68, 82-87.

29 Ibid., pp. 65, 99.

30 Ibid., p. 88.

31 Ibid., pp. 91-92.

32 Ibid., pp. 94, 96.

33 Ibid., p. 106; Connor, pp. 232-33.

34 Blake, pp. 71-72.

Chapter II

1 Arthur Ikin, *Texas* (London: Sherwood, Gilbert, and Piper, 1841); Webb and Carroll, 1:874 ("Arthur Ikin").

2 Webb and Carroll, 1:948 ("William Kennedy").

3 Wilbur Stanley Shepperson, *British Emigration to North America* (Oxford: Basil Blackwell, 1957), pp. 30-31, 45, 168.

4 Ernest Cabe Jr., "A Sketch of the Life of James Hamilton Cator," *Panhandle-Plains Historical Review* VI (1933): 40.

5 Ikin, p. 53.

6 Matilda Charlotte Houstoun, *Texas and the Gulf of Mexico* (Philadelphia: G.B. Zieber and Co., 1845), I: 113.

7 Billington, p. 64.

8 Ibid., pp. 37-38.

9 Charlotte Erickson, *Invisible Immigrants* (London: London School of Economics and Political Science, n.d.), pp. 20-22, 46.

10 Philip Graham, ed., "Texas Memoirs of Amelia E. Barr," *Southwestern Historical Quarterly* LXIX, 4 (April 1966): 493.

11 Wilbur Stanley Shepperson, *The Promotion of British Emigration by Agents for American Lands, 1840-1860* (Reno: University of Nevada Press, 1954), p. 185.

12 Edward Smith, *Account of a Journey through Northeastern Texas* (London: Hamilton, Adams, and Co., 1849); reprinted in *East Texas Historical Journal* VII, 1 (March 1969); VII, 2 (October 1969); VIII, 1 (March 1970); VII, 2: 103.

13 Shepperson, *Promotion of British Emigration*, p. 48.

14 Amelia E. Barr, *All the Days of My Life* (New York: D. Appleton and Co., 1913), p. 232.

15 Erickson, "English," p. 327.

16 Erickson, *Invisible Immigrants*, p. 46.

17 Isabel Holdsworth Simmons, "The Holdsworth Family in Texas," *Oldtimers: Their Own Stories*, ed. Florence Finley (Uvalde, Tex.: Hornsby Press, 1939), p. 146.

18 Ibid.

19 Erickson, *Invisible Immigrants*, pp. 65-66; Flossie Lill et al., "Diary of Five Sisters," *A Time to Purpose: A Chronicle of Carson County*, ed. Mrs. Ralph E. Randel (Seagraves, Tex.: Pioneer Publishers, 1966), p. 94.

[20] Simmons, p. 147.

[21] Lill, p. 95.

[22] Dotty Jones, *A Search for Opportunity: A History of Hansford County* (Gruver, Tex.: Jones Publishing Co., 1965), p. 68.

[23] Erickson, *Invisible Immigrants*, p. 57.

[24] Robert H. Williams, *With the Border Ruffians*, ed. E.W. Williams (London: John Murray, 1907; reprinted, Lincoln: University of Nebraska Press, 1982), p. 206.

[25] Richard Billsboro, San Antonio *Texas Sun* VI, 30 (April 1880): 1.

[26] Ibid., R. Luke.

[27] Quoted in Shepperson, *British Emigration to North America*, p. 178.

[28] Erickson, *Invisible Immigrants*, p. 29.

[29] Erickson, "English," pp. 320-23.

[30] Shepperson, *British Emigration to North America*, p. 31.

[31] Ralph A. Wooster, "Foreigners in the Principal Towns of Ante-Bellum Texas," *Southwestern Historical Quarterly* LXV, 2 (October 1962): 209.

[32] Homer L. Kerr, "Migration into Texas, 1860-1880," *Southwestern Historical Quarterly* LXX, 2 (October 1966): 203.

[33] Erickson, *Invisible Immigrants*, p. 15; Erickson, "English," p. 333.

[34] Shepperson, *British Emigration to North America*, p. 56.

[35] Ibid., p. 60.

[36] Ibid., p. 29.

[37] Ibid., p. 41.

[38] Shepperson, *Promotion of British Emigration*, p. 43.

[39] Maybelle Virginia Glasgow Stone, "Immigration to Texas, 1836-1845" (M.A. thesis, The University of Texas at Austin, 1938), p. 130; Shepperson, *British Emigration to North America*, pp. 172-75.

[40] Shepperson, *British Emigration to North America*, pp. 51, 170-71.

[41] Shepperson, *Promotion of British Emigration*, pp. 53-54.

[42] Ibid.

[43] Smith, VIII, 2: 101.

[44] Shepperson, *British Emigration to North America*, pp. 176-77.

[45] Ibid., pp. 86-93, 103, 176; Dorothy Waties Renick, "The City of Kent," *Southwestern Historical Quarterly* XXIX, 1 (July 1925): 51-65.

[46] Smith, VII, 1 (March 1969): 35-37, 46-47, 80-83.

[47] Shepperson, *British Emigration to North America*, p. 67.

[48] Ibid., p. 69.

49 Renick, pp. 55-57.

50 Ibid., pp. 54-55.

51 Ibid., p. 54.

52 Ibid., pp. 62-63.

53 Ibid., pp. 64-65.

The Chroniclers

1 Kennedy, p. 48.

2 Ibid.

3 Hooten, pp. 41-42.

4 Ibid., p. 73.

5 Ibid., p. ix.

6 Mary Lee Spence, p. 178; Shepperson, *British Emigration to North America*, p. 178.

7 Mary Lee Spence, p. 180.

8 Fredrick Marryat, *Diary in America*, 3 vols. (London: Longmans, 1839), II: 43, 50.

9 Ibid., I: 132.

10 R. Henderson Shuffler, "Books: Old and New," *Texas Parade*, October 1966, p. 50.

11 Ibid.

12 Maillard, pp. iii-iv.

13 Ibid., p. 206.

14 Pratt, p. viii.

15 Ibid., p. 95.

16 Ibid., p. 105.

17 Maillard, p. xiii.

18 Kennedy, p. v.

19 Beatrice Gay, *"Into the Setting Sun": A History of Coleman County* (Santa Anna, Tex.: Gay [?], 1936), p. 58.

20 William Bollaert, "Notes on the Coast Region of the Texan Territory," *Journal of the Royal Geographic Society* XIII (1844): 341; Mary Lee Spence, p. 166.

21 Bollaert, "Notes," p. 341.

22 Ibid., pp. 346, 354.

23 Hollon and Butler, p. 1.

24 Houstoun, II: 202-3.

25 Ibid., p. 226.

[26] Matilda Charlotte Houstoun, *Hesperos* (London), II: 120-21.

[27] Houstoun, *Texas and the Gulf of Mexico* II: 271.

[28] Marilyn McAdams Sibley, "The Queen's Lady in Texas," *East Texas Historical Journal* VI, 2 (October 1968): 109-16.

[29] Sibley, p. 115.

[30] Hooten, p. 54.

[31] Barr, pp. 181-83.

[32] Ibid., p. 181.

Chapter III

[1] Erickson, *Invisible Immigrants*, p. 19.

[2] Erickson, "English," p. 332.

[3] Charles Hooten, *St. Louis' Isle, or Texiana* (London: Simmons and Ward, 1847), p. 25.

[4] William Bollaert, "Arrival in Texas in 1842 . . .," *Colburn's United Service Magazine* (November 1846), p. 344.

[5] Ikin, p. 60.

[6] Erickson, *Invisible Immigrants*, p. 40.

[7] Ibid., pp. 51-54.

[8] Ibid., p. 55.

[9] Barr, p. 207.

[10] Erickson, *Invisible Immigrants*, pp. 3, 64.

[11] Pratt, *Galveston Island*, p. 13.

[12] Houstoun, I: 124.

[13] Cabe, pp. 22-23.

[14] Barr, p. 197.

[15] John Edgar, letter to editor of the Newcastle *Chronicle*, reprinted in *Texas Siftings* (Austin) I, 36 (January 14, 1882).

[16] Blake, p. 81.

[17] Houstoun, pp. 183-84.

[18] Blake, p. 80.

[19] Walter Lord, ed., *The Fremantle Diary* (Boston: Little, Brown and Company, 1954), p. 47.

[20] Maillard, pp. 202-6.

[21] Fredrick Marryat, *Narrative of the Travels and Adventures of Monsieur Violet* (London: Longman, Brown, and Green, 1843), p. 44.

[22] Pratt, p. 95.

23 Lord, p. 17.

24 Hooten, p. 138.

25 Lord, p. 8.

26 Mary Lee Spence, "British Impressions of Texas and the Texans," *Southwestern Historical Quarterly* LXX, 2 (October 1966): 177.

27 Smith, VII, 1: 33.

28 Hooten, p. 23.

29 Lord, p. 25.

30 Ibid., p. 20.

31 Pratt, p. 95.

32 Marryat, p. 55.

33 Smith, VII, 2:102.

34 Ibid.

35 Pratt, p. 37.

36 Featherstonhaugh, II: 157.

37 Lord, p. 46.

38 Ibid., pp. 53-54.

39 W. Eugene Hollon and Ruth Lapham Butler, eds., *William Bollaert's Texas* (Norman: University of Oklahoma Press, 1956), p. 340.

40 Maillard, p. 4.

41 Hollon and Butler, pp. 139-40.

42 Pratt, pp. 22, 148.

43 Houstoun, II: 272.

44 Barr, p. 207.

45 Houstoun, II: 272; Marion Day Mullins, *The First Census of Texas* (Washington, D.C.: National Genealogical Society, 1959).

46 Lord, p. 35.

47 Houstoun, II: 266.

48 Hollon and Butler, p. 140.

49 Maillard, p. 222.

50 Pratt, pp. 39-40.

51 Smith, VII, 2: 102.

52 Houstoun, II: 220.

53 Barr, p. 185.

54 Pratt, p. 18.

55 Hooten, p. 102.

56 Erickson, *Invisible Immigrants*, p. 30.

⁵⁷ Erickson, "English," p. 334; Erickson, *Invisible Immigrants*, p. 68.

⁵⁸ Lord, p. 49.

⁵⁹ Williams, p. 61.

⁶⁰ Barr, p. 206.

⁶¹ Featherstonhaugh, II: 170.

⁶² Houstoun, II: 226-27.

⁶³ Hooten, pp. 98-110.

⁶⁴ Erickson, *Invisible Immigrants*, pp. 73-74.

⁶⁵ Graham, p. 482.

⁶⁶ Erickson, *Invisible Immigrants*, p. 47.

⁶⁷ W.G. Kinsbury, quoted in San Antonio *Texas Sun* VI, 30 (April 1880): 1.

Chapter IV

[1] Barr, p. 227.

[2] *The Colonial Magazine* (January 1841), quoted in Shepperson, *Promotion of British Emigration*, p. 48.

[3] Erickson, *Invisible Immigrants*, pp. 75-76.

[4] Williams, pp. xvi, 55-64, 74-88, 157-65.

[5] Quoted in Erickson, *Invisible Immigrants*, p. 76.

[6] Barr, p. 221.

[7] Williams, pp. 148, 163, 165, 229, 319, 396, *passim*.

[8] Lord, pp. 7, 26, 44, 46.

[9] Ezra Warner, *Generals in Gray* (Baton Rouge: Louisiana State University Press, 1959), pp. 328-29; Webb and Carroll, 2:871 ("Thomas N. Waul").

[10] Leon Mitchell, "Camp Ford: Confederate Military Prison," *Southwestern Historical Quarterly* LXVI, 1 (July 1962): 14.

[11] Graham, p. 482.

[12] Barr, pp. 242-49; Graham, p. 483.

[13] Graham, pp. 483, 485; Barr, p. 245.

[14] Graham, p. 487.

[15] Barr, p. 250.

[16] Graham, pp. 488-89.

[17] Barr, pp. 259-61, 268.

[18] Pearl Hendricks, "Quaint Booklet Tells of Founding of Confederate Home," *Houston Chronicle Art Gravure Magazine* (February 20, 1944), p. 2.

[19] Williams, pp. 410-11.

20 John Baumann, "On a Western Ranche," *The Fortnightly Review* XLVII (April 1, 1887): 517-18.

21 Webb and Carroll, 1:8 ("Adobe Walls").

22 Ibid., 2:328 ("Palo Duro Canyon").

23 Lowell H. Harrison, "Some British Views of Texas, 1877-1878," *Texana* VI, 2 (Summer 1968): 122.

24 Ibid., p. 123.

25 Estelle Tinkler, "History of the Rocking Chair Brand," *Panhandle-Plains Historical Review* XV (1942):5.

26 W.H. King, "Report of the Adjutant General of the State of Texas," *Reports of Departments and State Institutions of Texas* (Galveston: A.H. Belo and Co., 1881), p. 27.

27 *Deed Records*, Collingsworth County, V: 165.

28 James Macdonald, *Food from the Far West* (London: William P. Nimmo, 1878), pp. 26-29.

29 E.E. Dale, *The Range Cattle Industry* (Norman: University of Oklahoma Press, 1930), p. 98.

30 Lowell H. Harrison, ed., "Wintering in the Palo Duro Canyon, 1876-1877," *Panhandle-Plains Historical Review* XXXVIII (1965): 45.

31 n.a., "A Glimpse of the West," *Blackwoods Edinburgh Magazine* CXXXV (June 1884): 762.

32 n.a., "Ranche Life in the Far West," *MacMillan's Magazine* XLVIII (August 1883): 293.

33 Billington, pp. 51-52.

34 Erickson, "English," pp. 325-26; Erickson, *Invisible Immigrants*, p. 110.

35 L.F. Sheffy, "British Capital and the Cattle Business," *The Cattleman* XVI, 10 (March 1930): 57.

36 W. Baillie Grohman, "Cattle Ranches in the Far West," *Cornhill Magazine* XXVIII (n.s.): 441.

37 Billington, p. 46.

38 Arlene Pickett, *Historic Liberty County* (n.p: Tardy Publishing Company, [1936]), pp. 45-47.

39 W.G. Sutherland, "Adams Brothers, Trans-Nueces Pioneers," *The Cattleman*, June 1930, pp. 17-21.

40 Arthur H. Patterson, "Camp Life on the Prairies," *MacMillan's Magazine* XLIX (January 1884): 172.

41 Ibid.

42 Ibid.

43 Ibid., p. 169.

44 "Ranche Life in the Far West," p. 293.

45 Ibid., p. 297.

46 Roland Tappan Berthoff, *British Immigrants in Industrial America: 1790-1950* (Cambridge, Mass.: Harvard University Press, 1953), p. 117.

47 *Texas Almanac, 1982-1983* (Dallas: A.H. Belo Corp., 1981), p. 526.

48 *Anglo-American Times*, November 16, 1877, p. 129.

49 Frank Collinson, *Life in the Saddle*, ed. and arr. Mary Whatley Clarke (Norman: University of Oklahoma Press, 1963), p. 4.

50 Ibid., quoted in dust jacket copy.

51 Earl Pomeroy, *In Search of the Golden West* (New York: Alfred A. Knopf, 1957), pp. 83-89.

52 J. Frank Dobie, *A Texan in England* (Boston: Little, Brown, 1945; reprinted, Austin: University of Texas Press, 1980), p. 264.

53 Billington, pp. 172-73.

54 Julius H. Matthey, "Reminiscences of Fifty Years, 1872-1922," p. 53, ms. in the Library of the Daughters of the Republic of Texas at the Alamo, San Antonio.

55 [John Baumann], "The Cow-Boy at Home," *Cornhill Magazine* VII (September 1886): 295.

56 Edgar, n.p.

57 "The Cow-Boy at Home," p. 301.

58 Ibid.

59 Grohman, p. 447.

60 Lord, pp. 19, 34, 58.

61 Grohman, p. 447.

62 "The Cow-Boy at Home," p. 299.

63 Grohman, p. 457.

64 "The Cow-Boy at Home," p. 301.

65 Ibid.

66 Baumann, "Western Ranche," p. 516.

67 Harrison, p. 46.

68 Edgar, n.p.

69 Patterson, p. 172.

70 "The Cow-Boy at Home," p. 298.

71 Patterson, p. 172.

[72] Estelle Tinkler, *Archibald John Writes the Rocking Chair Ranche Letters* (Burnet, Tex.: Nortex Press, 1979), pp. 149, 211-12.

[73] Ester Felt Bentley, "A Conversation with Mr. Rollins," *The Princeton University Library Chronicle* IX, 4 (June 1948): 189. Quoted in J. Frank Dobie, "Introduction," Charles Siringo, *A Texas Cowboy* (Lincoln: University of Nebraska Press, 1970), p. xxvi.

[74] J. Evetts Haley, *The XIT Ranch of Texas* (Norman: University of Oklahoma Press, 1929; 1953; 1967), pp. 72-74.

[75] Ibid., p. 76.

[76] Webb and Carroll, 2:940 ("XIT Ranch").

[77] Ibid., 2:1 ("LX Ranch").

[78] Ibid., 1:5 ("John George Adair"); conversation with Byron Price, April 20, 1982.

[79] n.a. *A History of Collingsworth County* (Wellington, Tex.: Leader Printing Co., 1925), p. 159; Virginia Browder, *Donley County, Land of Promise* (Burnet, Tex.: Nortex Press, 1975), pp. 80-82.

[80] Lester Fields Sheffy, *The Francklyn Land and Cattle Company* (Austin: University of Texas Press, 1963), p. 7.

[81] Tinkler, "Rocking Chair Brand," p. 21; Sheffy, "British Capital and the Cattle Business," p. 57.

[82] Jeanne Lively, "Becoming a Legend," *This is West Texas* (September-October 1971), p. 11.

[83] James I. Fenton, "Big Spring's Amazing Tenderfoot: The Earl of Aylesford," *West Texas Historical Journal* LV (1979): 135.

[84] John Ashton, "Billy Anson and the Quarter Horse," *The Cattleman* XXXIII, 4 (September 1946): 33-37.

[85] Walter Gann, "War Horses for the British," *Old West* (Spring 1973), pp. 20-23, 68-70.

[86] Robert M. Denhardt, "Greatest of Early Texas Quarter Horse Breeders," *The Cattleman* XXVII, 5 (October 1940): 73-75; Robert M. Denhardt, "Anson Talks about Quarter Horses," *The Cattleman* XXXVII, 4 (September 1940): 55, 138-44; Robert M. Denhardt, "William Anson: Texas' Number One Breeder of Quarter Horses," *The Cattleman* XLVIII, 4 (September 1961): 36-37, 64-65.

[87] Mrs. Ralph E. Randel, ed., "Cecil Victor Payne Buckler," *A Time to Purpose: A Chronicle of Carson County* (Seagraves, Tex.: Pioneer Publishers, 1966), pp. 124-37.

[88] R.D. Holt, "The Busk Ranch in Coleman County," *The Cattleman* XXVI, 6 (November 1939): 28-44.

89 Tinkler, *Archibald John Writes*, pp. 5-6; Tinkler, "Rocking Chair Brand," p. 21.

90 Fred Arrington, *A History of Dickens County: Ranches and Rolling Plains* (n.p.: Nortex Offset Publications, 1971), p. 97.

91 Unidentified typescript in The Institute of Texan Cultures' vertical files.

92 Frank X. Tolbert, "Tolbert's Texas: Why His Lordship Stared at Dinner," unidentified newspaper clipping in The Institute of Texan Cultures' files.

93 Copy of page from unidentified book, The Institute of Texan Cultures' files.

94 Unidentified typescript, The Institute of Texan Cultures' files.

95 Will James, *Cow Country* (New York: Charles Scribner's Sons, 1929), p. 67; Grohman, p. 457.

96 Baumann, "Western Ranche," p. 533.

97 Ibid.; Haley, p. 211.

98 Webb and Carroll, 1:28 ("Alien Land Law"); C.W. Raines, ed., *Speeches and State Papers of James Stephen Hogg* (Austin: State Printing Co., 1905).

99 Richard Harding Davis, *The West from a Car Window* (New York: Harper and Brothers, 1892), p. 132.

100 J. Fred Rippy, "British Investment in Texas Land and Livestock," *Southwestern Historical Quarterly* LVIII, 3 (January 1955): 338.

101 Gene M. Gressley, "Broker to the British: Francis Smith and Company," *Southwestern Historical Quarterly* LXXI, 1 (July 1967): 22.

102 Rippy, p. 339.

103 Simmons, p. 151; Smith, VIII, 1: 42.

104 Lester F. Sheffy, "British Pounds and British Purebreds," *Panhandle-Plains Historical Review* XI (March 1938): 66.

105 Ibid., p. 67.

Chapter V

1 Pomeroy, p. 83.

2 Cabe, pp. 13-23; Lowell H. Harrison, "Adobe Walls Area, 1874," *Panhandle-Plains Historical Review* XXXVI (1963): 40-46; Dotty Jones, *A Search for Opportunity*, pp. 59-71.

3 Don Rickey, *Forty Miles a Day on Beans and Hay* (Norman: University of Oklahoma Press, 1963), p. 18.

4 Colin Rickards, "The Cowboy from Yorkshire," *True West* (May-June 1969), pp. 21, 62-63; Colin Rickards, "Gunfighter from Yorkshire," *Frontier Times* (October-November 1963), pp. 22-23, 66-67.

5 N.A. Jennings, *A Texas Ranger* (Dallas: Southwest Press, 1930), p. 227; C.L. Sonnichsen, *I'll Die Before I'll Run* (New York: Harper and Row, 1951), pp. 71-78.

[6] Paul Trachtman, *The Gunfighters* (Alexandria, Va.: Time-Life Books, 1974), pp. 67, 113-18.

[7] Lawrence H. Warburton Jr., "Henry Marcus Holmes," *Texas Bar Journal* 42, 8 (September 1979): 710-14.

[8] Walter B. King Jr., "James E. Thompson, M.B., B.S., F.R.C.S. (Eng.), F.A.S.C., L.L.D., First President of the Texas Surgical Society," Presidential Address to the Texas Surgical Society, October 2, 1967. Typescript in "James E. Thompson" file at The Institute of Texan Cultures.

[9] Webb and Carroll, 2:774 (K.H. Aynesworth, "James E. Thompson").

[10] Grafton Burke, "From Texas to Alaska," *The Alaskan Churchman*, February 1921, pp. 39-41; George Edwards, *Pioneer at Law* (New York: W.W. Norton, 1974), pp. 21-24.

[11] Vernon Gladden Spence, *Colonel Morgan Jones* (Norman: University of Oklahoma Press, 1971).

[12] Mary Carolyn Hollers Juston, *Alfred Giles* (San Antonio: Trinity University Press, 1972).

[13] Davis, pp. 132-35.

[14] Lillie Langtry, *The Days I Knew* (New York: George H. Doran Co., 1925), pp. 189-99.

[15] Webb and Carroll, 2:18 ("Joseph Lancaster"); Hobart Huson, "J. Lancaster, Pioneer Editor," Sinton *Enterprise*, October 1928.

[16] Webb and Carroll, 1:476 (Sam Acherson, "George B. Dealey"); John E. Rosser, "G.B. Dealey of the *News*," *Southwest Review* XXXI, 4 (Autumn 1946): 327-32; *Texas Almanac, 1970-1971*, p. 33.

[17] Webb and Carroll, 1:476 (Wayne Gard, "James Quayle Dealey").

[18] Ibid., 1:870 ("Henry Hutchings").

[19] Mabel Major, "The Man Who Wrote 'Lasca,' " *Southwest Review* XXXVI (Autumn 1951): 301.

[20] J. Frank Dobie, *The Longhorns* (New York: Bramhall House, 1941), p. 128.

[21] John A. Lomax, *Adventures of a Ballad Hunter* (New York: Macmillan Company, 1947), pp. 24-25, 84.

[22] Major, pp. 301-5.

[23] Webb and Carroll, 3:576 ("William John Marsh").

[24] Rosalie Fincher, "The History of Liberty County" (M.A. thesis, The University of Texas, 1937).

[25] E.E. Risien, San Saba *Star*, September 26, 1940.

[26] Peter D. Franklin, "Around the Plaza," *San Antonio Light*, September 25, 1972, p. 10-A.

27 "Irish Lord Carried Flag in Survey of San Angelo," San Angelo *Standard Times*, August 29, 1954; "Angelo Link Suggested to *Virginian* Novel," *Standard Times*, November 1, 1970; "Irish Nobleman Who Aided British During World War Dies Here," *Standard Times*, March 23, 1936.

28 Stephen Earll, "Lt. George Kelly," San Antonio *Express News Sunday Magazine*, November 3, 1974, p. 5.

29 *1980 Census of Population*, Vol. I, *Characteristics of the Population*, Chap. C, *General, Social and Economic Characteristics*, Part 45: *Texas*, Table 63 (Washington, D.C.: Dept. of Commerce, Bureau of the Census, 1983).

30 "Graham Greene," Dallas *News*, August 24, 1953.

31 Jack Maguire, "The British Invasion," *Southwest Airlines Magazine* XIII, 11 (June 1984): 48.

32 Lyndon B. Johnson quoted in Dallas *Morning News*, April 30, 1961.

The Welsh in Texas

1 Shepperson, *British Emigration to North America*, pp. 31-33; Erickson, "English," p. 320; Alan Conway, *The Welsh in America* (Minneapolis: University of Minnesota Press, 1961), pp. 118-19.

2 Conway, pp. 257-58.

3 Ibid., pp. 151-55.

4 Ibid., pp. 258-59.

Bibliography

Adams, Ephraim Douglas. *British Interests and Activities in Texas, 1838-1846.* Baltimore: Johns Hopkins Press, 1910; reprinted, Gloucester, Mass.: Peter Smith, 1963.

Arrington, Fred. *A History of Dickens County: Ranches and Rolling Plains.* n.p.: Nortex Offset Publications, 1971.

Bancroft, Hubert Howe. *History of the North Mexican States and Texas, 1801-1889.* San Francisco: History Company, Publishers, 1889.

Barr, Amelia E. *All the Days of My Life: An Autobiography; The Red Leaves of a Human Heart.* New York: D. Appleton and Co., 1913.

Berthoff, Rowland Tappan. *British Immigrants in Industrial America: 1790-1950.* Cambridge, Mass.: Harvard University Press, 1953.

Billington, Ray Allen. *Land of Savagery, Land of Promise: The European Image of the American Frontier.* New York: W.W. Norton and Company, 1981.

Blake, Clagette. *Charles Elliot, R.N., 1801-1875: A Servant of Britain Overseas.* London: Cleaver-Hume Press, 1960.

Browder, Virginia. *Donley Country: Land of Promise.* Burnet, Tex.: Nortex Press, 1975.

Buckingham, James Silk. *The Slave States of America.* 2 vols. London, 1842.

Catlin, George. *Letters and Notes on the North American Indians.* New York: Wiley and Putnam, 1841.

Channing, William Ellery. *Thoughts on the Evils of a Spirit of Conquest and on Slavery: A Letter on the Annexation of Texas to the United States.* London, 1837.

Collinson, Frank. *Life in the Saddle.* Ed. and arr. Mary Whatley Clarke. Norman: University of Oklahoma Press, 1963.

Connor, Seymour V. *Adventure in Glory: The Saga of Texas, 1836-1849.* Austin: Steck-Vaughn, 1965.

__________. *The Peters Colony of Texas.* Austin: Texas State Historical Association, 1957.

Conway, Alan. *The Welsh in America: Letters from the Immigrants.* Minneapolis: University of Minnesota Press, 1961.

Dale, E.E. *The Range Cattle Industry.* Norman: University of Oklahoma Press, 1930.

David, Richard, ed. *Hakluyt's Voyages.* Boston: Houghton Mifflin Company, 1981.

Davis, Richard Harding. *The West from a Car Window.* New York: Harper and Brothers, 1892.

Dobie, J. Frank. *The Longhorns.* New York: Bramhall House, 1941.

__________. *A Texan in England.* Boston: Little, Brown, 1945; reprinted, Austin:

University of Texas Press, 1980.

Dunae, Patrick A. *Gentlemen Emigrants: From the British Public Schools to Canadian Frontier.* Seattle: University of Washington Press, 1982.

Erickson, Charlotte. *Invisible Immigrants: The Adaptation of English and Scottish Immigrants in Nineteenth-Century America.* London: London School of Economics and Political Science, n.d.

Featherstonhaugh, George William. *Excursions Through the Slave States, from Washington on the Potomac to the Frontier of Mexico.* 2 vols. London: J. Murray, 1844.

Finkelstein, Mrs. Dave. *John and Margaret Hallett, American Pioneers, Founders of Hallettsville, Texas.* Hallettsville, Tex.: Hallettsville *Tribune,* 1951.

Fremantle, Arthur James Lyon, Lt. Col. *The Fremantle Diary: Being the Journal of Lieutenant Colonel Arthur James Lyon Fremantle, Coldstream Guards, on his Three Months in the Southern States.* Ed. Walter Lord. Boston: Little, Brown and Company, 1954.

Haley, J. Evetts. *The XIT Ranch of Texas.* Norman: University of Oklahoma Press, 1929; 1953; 1967.

Hartmann, Edward George. *Americans from Wales.* Boston: Christopher Publishing House, 1967.

Holden, William Curry. *The Espuela Land and Cattle Company: A Study of a Foreign Owned Ranch in Texas.* Austin: Texas State Historical Association, 1970.

Hollon, W. Eugene, and Ruth Lapham Butler, eds. *William Bollaert's Texas.* Norman: University of Oklahoma Press, 1956.

Hooten, Charles. *St. Louis' Isle, or Texiana; With Additional Observations Made in the United States and Canada.* London: Simmons and Ward, 1847.

Horgan, Paul. *Great River: The Rio Grande in North American History.* New York: Holt, Rinehart and Winston, 1954.

Houstoun, Matilda Charlotte. *Texas and the Gulf of Mexico; or Yachting in the New World.* Philadelphia: G.B. Zieber and Co., 1845.

Ikin, Arthur. *Texas: Its History, Topography, Agriculture, Commerce, and General Statistics; To Which is Added a Copy of the Treaty of Commerce Entered Into by the Republic of Texas and Great Britain; Designed for the Use of the British Merchant, and as a Guide to Emigrants.* London: Sherwood, Gilbert, and Piper, 1841.

James, Will. *Cow Country.* New York: Charles Scribner's Sons, 1929.

Jennings, N.A. *A Texas Ranger.* Dallas: Southwest Press, 1930.

Juston, Mary Carolyn Hollers. *Alfred Giles: An English Architect in Texas and Mexico.* San Antonio: Trinity University Press, 1972.

Kennedy, William. *Texas: Its Geography, Natural History, and Topography.* New York: Benjamin and Young, John Street, 1847.

————. *Texas: The Rise, Progress, and Prospects of the Republic of Texas.* 2 vols.

London: R. Hastings, 1841.

Kerr, W.G. *Scottish Capital on the American Credit Frontier.* Austin: Texas State Historical Association, 1976.

Langtry, Lillie [Lady DeBathe]. *The Days I Knew.* New York: George H. Doran Co., 1925.

Lathrop, Barnes F. *Migration into East Texas, 1835-1860: A Study from the United States Census.* Austin: Texas Historical Association, 1949.

Life in the South; From the Commencement of the War by a Blockaded British Subject, vol. II. London: Chapman and Hall, 1863.

Lomax, John A. *Adventures of a Ballad Hunter.* New York: Macmillan Company, 1947.

Lord, Walter, ed. *The Fremantle Diary: Being the Journal of Lieutenant Colonel Arthur James Lyon Fremantle, Coldstream Guards, on his Three Months in the Southern States.* Boston: Little, Brown and Company, 1954.

Lunt, W.E. *History of England.* 4th ed. New York: Harper and Row, Publishers, 1957.

Macdonald, James. *Food from the Far West.* London: William P. Nimmo, 1878.

Maillard, N. Doran. *The History of the Republic of Texas.* London: Smith, Elder, and Company, 1842.

Marryat, Fredrick. *Diary in America, with Remarks on Its Institutions.* 3 vols. London: Longmans, 1839.

__________. *Narrative of the Travels and Adventures of Monsieur Violet, in California, Sonora, and Western Texas.* 3 vols. London: Longman, Brown, and Green, 1843.

Minig, D.W. *Imperial Texas: An Interpretive Essay in Cultural Geography.* Austin: University of Texas Press, 1969.

Mullins, Marion Day. *The First Census of Texas, 1829-1836, to Which Are Added Texas Citizenship Lists, 1821-1845 and Other Early Records of the Republic of Texas.* Washington, D.C.: National Genealogical Society, 1959.

Pender, Rose. *A Lady's Experience in the Wild West in 1883. In Search of a Round-up.* London: Tucker [1889].

Pomeroy, Earl. *In Search of the Golden West: The Tourist in Western America.* New York: Alfred A. Knopf, 1957.

Pratt, Willis W., ed. *Galveston Island, or, A Few Months off the Coast of Texas: The Journal of Francis C. Sheridan.* Austin: University of Texas Press, 1954.

Rayburn, John C., and Virginia Kemp Rayburn, eds. *Century of Conflict: 1821-1913; Incidents in the Lives of William Neale and William Alfred Neale, Early Settlers in South Texas.* Waco: Texian Press, 1966.

Richardson, Ruppert N. *Colonel Edward M. House: The Texas Years, 1858-1912.* Abilene: Hardin-Simmons University Press, 1964.

Rickey, Don. *Forty Miles a Day on Beans and Hay.* Norman: University of Oklahoma Press, 1963.

Rickards, Colin. *Bowler Hats and Stetsons: Stories of Englishmen in the Wild West.* New York: Bonanza Books, 1967.

St. John, Percy Bolingbroke. *Enchanted Rock: A Comanche Legend.* London: Hayes and Adam, 1846.

__________. *Mary Rock; or, My Adventures in Texas.* London, 1847.

Sealsfield, Charles. *The Americans As They Are: Described in a Tour Through the Valley of the Mississippi.* London, 1828.

Sheffy, Lester Fields. *The Francklyn Land and Cattle Company.* Austin: University of Texas Press, 1963.

Shepperson, Wilbur Stanley. *British Emigration to North America: Projects and Opinions in the Early Victorian Period.* Oxford: Basil Blackwell, 1957.

__________. *The Promotion of British Emigration by Agents for American Lands, 1840-1860.* Reno: University of Nevada Press, 1954.

Sheridan, Francis C. *Galveston Island; or, a Few Months off the Coast of Texas.* Ed. Willis W. Pratt. Austin: University of Texas Press, 1954.

Smith, Edward. *Account of a Journey through Northeastern Texas.* London: Hamilton, Adams, and Co., 1849; reprinted in *East Texas Historical Journal* VII, 1 (March 1969); VII, 2 (October 1969); VIII, 1 (March 1970).

Sonnichsen, C.L. *I'll Die Before I'll Run: The Story of the Great Texas Feuds.* New York: Harper and Row, 1951.

Spence, Clark C. *British Investments and the American Mining Frontier, 1860-1901.* Ithaca, N.Y.: Cornell University Press, 1958.

Spence, Vernon Gladden. *Colonel Morgan Jones: Grand Old Man of Texas Railroading.* Norman: University of Oklahoma Press, 1971.

Sweet, Alex E., and J. Armoy Knox. *On a Mexican Mustang through Texas.* London: Chatto and Windus, 1905.

Trachtman, Paul. *The Gunfighters.* Alexandria, Va.: Time-Life Books, 1974.

Tinkler, Estelle. *Archibald John Writes the Rocking Chair Ranche Letters.* Burnet, Tex.: Nortex Press, 1979.

Unwin, Raymer. *The Defeat of John Hawkins: A Biography of His Third Slaving Voyage.* New York: Macmillan Company, 1960.

Urquhart, David. *Annexation of the Texas, A Case of War Between England and the United States.* London: James Maynard, 1844.

Warner, Ezra. *Generals in Gray.* Baton Rouge: Louisiana State University Press, 1959.

Webb, Walter Prescott, and H. Bailey Carroll, eds. *Handbook of Texas,* 3 vols. (Austin: Texas State Historical Association, 1952, 1976.

Williams, Robert H. *With the Border Ruffians: Memories of the Far West, 1852-1868.* Ed. E.W. Williams. London: John Murray, 1907; reprinted, Lincoln: University of Nebraska Press, 1982.

Articles

Adams, Paul. "Amelia Barr in Texas." *Southwestern Historical Quarterly* XLIX, 3 (January 1946): 361-73.

Ashton, John. "Pronger Brothers: How Two English Lads Established a Successful Ranching Business in the Texas Panhandle." *The Cattleman* XXXVII, 8 (January 1951): 17, 42-52.

[Baumann, John.] "The Cow-Boy at Home." *Cornhill Magazine* VII (September 1886).

Baumann, John. "On a Western Ranche." *The Fortnightly Review* XLVII (April 1, 1887): 516-33.

Bentley, Ester Felt. "A Conversation with Mr. Rollins." *The Princeton University Library Chronicle* IX, 4 (June 1948): 189. Quoted in J. Frank Dobie, "Introduction," Charles Siringo, *A Texas Cowboy*. Lincoln: University of Nebraska Press, 1970.

Bollaert, William. "Arrival in Texas in 1842, and Cruise of the Lafitte." *Colburn's United Service Magazine*, November 1846, pp. 342-55.

————. "Notes on the Coast Region of the Texan Territory, Taken During a Visit in 1842." *Journal of the Royal Geographic Society* XIII (1844): 226-44.

Brasseaux, Carl A., and Richard E. Chandler. "The *Britain* Incident, 1769-1770: Anglo-Hispanic Tensions in the Western Gulf." *Southwestern Historical Quarterly* LXXXVII, 4 (April 1984): 357-58.

Cabe, Ernest, Jr. "A Sketch of the Life of James Hamilton Cator." *Panhandle-Plains Historical Review* VI (1933): 13-23.

Cabler, Marie Durham. "Unsung Hero, A Biography of George John Durham." *Texana*, pp. 177-86.

Connor, Seymour V. "Early Land Speculation in West Texas." *Southwestern Social Sciences Quarterly* VIII.

Conway, Alan. "Welsh Emigration to the United States." *Perspectives in American History* VII (1973). Ed. Donald Fleming and Bernard Balyn. Cambridge, Mass.: The Charles Warren Center for Studies in American History.

Cox, Isaac Joslin. "The Louisiana-Texas Frontier." *Quarterly of the Texas State Historical Association* X, 1 (July 1906): 35-65.

Debo, Augie. "An English View of the Wild West." *Panhandle-Plains Historical Review* VI (1933): 24-44.

Dobie, J. Frank. "The Tournament in Texas." *Rainbow in the Morning*, pp. 94-103. Ed. J. Frank Dobie. Publications of the Texas Folklore Society Number V. Reprinted, Hatboro, Pa.: Folklore Associates, 1965.

Erickson, Charlotte. "English." *Harvard Encyclopedia of American Ethnic Groups,* pp. 319-36. Ed. Stephen Thernstrom. Cambridge, Mass.: Harvard University Press, 1980.

Erickson, J.E. "Origins of the Texas Bill of Rights." *Southwestern Historical Quarterly* LXII, 4 (April 1959): 457-66.

Falconer, Thomas. "Notes of a Journey Through Texas and New Mexico, in the Years 1841 and 1842." *Journal of the Royal Geographical Society* XIII (1844): 199-226.

Fenton, James I. "Big Spring's Amazing Tenderfoot: The Earl of Aylesford." *West Texas Historical Journal* LV (1979): 135-48.

Gould, Lewis L., ed. "A Texan in London: A British Editor Lunches with Colonel Edward M. House, February 15, 1916." *Southwestern Historical Quarterly* LXXIV, 4 (April 1981): 427-34.

Graham, Philip, ed. "Texas Memoirs of Amelia E. Barr." *Southwestern Historical Quarterly* LXIX, 4 (April 1966): 473-98.

Gressley, Gene M. "Broker to the British: Francis Smith and Company." *Southwestern Historical Quarterly* LXXI, 1 (July 1967): 7-25.

Grohman, W. Baillie. "Cattle Ranches in the Far West." *Cornhill Magazine* XXVIII, n.s.

Harrison, Lowell H. "Some British Views of Texas, 1877-1878." *Texana* VI, 2 (Summer 1968): 122-39.

__________, ed. "Wintering in Palo Duro Canyon, 1876-1877." *Panhandle-Plains Historical Review* XXXVIII (1965): 45-51.

Hawkins, John. "A True Declaration of the Troublesome Voyage of M. John Hawkins to the Parts of Guinea and the West Indies, in the Years of our Lord 1567 and 1568." *Hakluyt's Voyages*, pp. 403-7. Ed. Richard David. Boston: Houghton Mifflin Co., 1981.

Hooten, Charles. "The Exploit of Moreno the Texan." *The New Monthly Magazine and Humorist*, 1845.

Huson, Hobart. "J. Lancaster, Pioneer Editor." Sinton, Tex., *Enterprise*, October 1928.

Ingram, David. "The Relation of David Ingram of Barking, in the Countie of Essex, Sayler." *The Principall Navigations, Voiages and Discoveries of the English Nation*, pp. 403-7. Ed. Richard Hakluyt. London: George Bishop, 1589; reprinted as *Hakluyt's Voyages*, Boston: Houghton Mifflin Company, 1981.

Kerr, Homer L. "Migration into Texas, 1860-1880." *Southwestern Historical Quarterly* LXX, 2 (October 1966): 184-203.

King, Walter B., Jr. "James E. Thompson, M.B., B.S., F.R.C.S. (Eng.), F.A.S.C., L.L.D., First President of the Texas Surgical Society." Presidential address of the Texas Surgical Society, October 2, 1967. Typescript in "James E.

Thompson" file at The Institute of Texan Cultures.

King, W.H. "Report of the Adjutant General of the State of Texas." *Reports of Departments and State Institutions of Texas.* Galveston: A.H. Belo and Co., 1881.

Lill, Flossie, Ruby, Maggie, Lydia and Nellie. "Diary of Five Sisters." *A Time to Purpose: A Chronicle of Carson County,* pp. 94-96. Ed. Mrs. Ralph E. Randel. n.p.: Pioneer Publishers, 1966.

Lively, Jeanne. "Becoming a Legend." *This is West Texas,* September-October 1971, pp. 11, 12, 22, 23.

Major, Mabel. "The Man Who Wrote 'Lasca.' " *Southwest Review* XXXVI (Autumn 1951): 298-305.

Mayfield, G.C. "Oldest Texas Ranger an Englishman." *San Antonio Light,* March 20, 1932.

Mitchell, Leon. "Camp Ford: Confederate Military Prison." *Southwestern Historical Quarterly* LXVI, 1 (July 1962): 1-16.

Patterson, Arthur H. "Camp Life on the Prairies." *MacMillan's Magazine* XLIX (January 1884): 171-81.

"Ranche Life in the Far West." *MacMillan's Magazine* XLVIII (August 1883): 293-98.

Renick, Dorothy Waties. "The City of Kent." *Southwestern Historical Quarterly* XXIX, 1 (July 1925): 51-65.

Richardson, Rupert N. "Edward M. House and the Governors." *Southwestern Historical Quarterly* LXI (1958): 51-65.

Richardson, T.C. "The A. LeGrand Survey for the Beales and Royella Grant." *West Texas Historical Association Year Book* XXXI (October 1955): 102-21.

Rickards, Colin. "The Cowboy from Yorkshire." *True West,* May-June 1969, pp. 20-21, 61-64.

_________. "Gunfighter from Yorkshire." *Frontier Times,* October-November 1963, pp. 22-23, 66-67.

Rippy, J. Fred. "British Investment in Texas Land and Livestock." *Southwestern Historical Quarterly* LVIII, 3 (January 1955): 331-41.

Rister, C.C. "The Rio Grande Colony." *Southwestern Historical Quarterly* XXV, 4 (July 1940): 429-41.

Rosser, John E. "G.B. Dealey of the *News." Southwest Review* XXXI, 4 (Autumn 1946): 327-32.

Sheffy, Lester F. "British Capital and the Cattle Business." *The Cattleman* XVI, 10 (March 1930): 53-68.

_________. "British Pounds and British Purebreds." *Panhandle-Plains Historical Review* XI (March 1938): 55-68.

————. "Colonel B.B. Grooms." *A Time to Purpose: A Chronicle of Carson Co.* Ed. Mrs. Ralph E. Randel. n.p.: Pioneer Publishers, 1966.

Shepperson, Wilbur S. "Some Plans for British Immigration to Texas in 1849 and 1850." *Southwestern Historical Quarterly* LXIII, 3 (January 1960): 439-49.

Shuffler, R. Henderson. "Books: Old and New." *Texas Parade*, October 1966, p. 50.

Sibley, Marilyn McAdams. "The Queen's Lady in Texas." *East Texas Historical Journal* VI, 2 (October 1968): 109-23.

Simmons, Isabel Holdsworth. "The Holdsworth Family in Texas." *Oldtimers: Their Own Stories*, pp. 145-57. Ed. Florence Fenley. Uvalde: The Hornsby Press, 1939.

Smith, Edward. "Account of a Journey Through Northeast Texas." *East Texas Historical Association* VII, 1 (March 1969): 28-59; VII, 2 (October 1969): 18-109; VIII, 1 (March 1970): 29-91.

Spence, Mary Lee. "British Impressions of Texas and the Texans." *Southwestern Historical Quarterly* LXX, 2 (October 1966): 163-83.

Sutherland, W.G. "Adams Brothers, Trans-Nueces Pioneers." *The Cattleman*, June 1930, pp. 17-21.

Tinkler, Estelle. "History of the Rocking Chair Brand." *Panhandle-Plains Historical Review* XV (1942): 1-96.

Urwitz, Marie Bennet. "Valentine Bennet." *The Quarterly of the State Historical Association* IX, 3 (January 1906): 145-56.

Warburton, Lawrence H., Jr. "Henry Marcus Holmes: A Texas Law Practice." *Texas Bar Journal* 42, 8 (September 1979): 709-15.

Wooster, Ralph A. "Foreigners in the Principal Towns of Ante-Bellum Texas." *Southwestern Historical Quarterly* LXV, 2 (October 1962): 208-20.

Worley, J.L. "The Diplomatic Relations of England and the Republic of Texas." *Quarterly of the Texas State Historical Association* IX, 1 (July 1905): 1-40.

Unpublished Manuscripts, Theses and Dissertations

Kerr, Homer Lee. "Migration into Texas, 1860-1880." Ph.D. dissertation, The University of Texas at Austin, 1953.

Majoribanks, A.J. "Rocking Chair Ranche Letters (Miscellaneous)." Manuscript in Panhandle-Plains Historical Museum, Canyon, Texas.

Matthey, Julius H. "Reminiscences of Fifty Years, 1872-1922." Manuscript in the Library of the Daughters of the Republic of Texas at the Alamo.

Stone, Maybelle Virginia Glasgow. "Immigration to Texas, 1836-1845." M.A. thesis, The University of Texas at Austin, 1938.

White, William Wilson. "Migration into West Texas, 1845-1860." M.A. thesis, The University of Texas at Austin, 1948.

Photo Credits

Credits from top to bottom are separated by dashes, left to right by semicolons.

Page   8 *Harper's New Monthly Magazine* (New York: Harper and Brothers, 1883), vol. 66, p. 224.

Page   9 David Ingram, *Across Aboriginal America: The Journey of Three Englishmen in 1568*, ed. Edward De Golyer (El Paso: Peripatetic Press, 1947).

Page 12 The Tate Gallery, London.

Page 15 *History of Texas—Together with a Biographical History of the Cities of Houston and Galveston* (Chicago: Lewis Publishing Company, 1895); Charles Seymour, ed., *The Intimate Papers of Colonel House* (Boston and New York, 1926-1928).

Page 16 Hallettsville Chamber of Commerce—Austin-Travis County Collection, Austin Public Library.

Page 17 Louis J. Wortham, *A History of Texas, From Wilderness to Commonwealth* (Fort Worth: Wortham-Molyneaux, 1924).

Page 22 Barker Texas History Center, The University of Texas at Austin.

Page 24 The Library of the Daughters of the Republic of Texas at the Alamo.

Page 26 Clagette Blake, *Charles Elliot, R.N., 1801-1875: A Servant of Britain Overseas* (London: Cleaver-Hume Press, 1960).

Page 28 London Museum.

Page 32 Barker Texas History Center, The University of Texas at Austin.

Page 33 Marcius Willson, *American History: Comprising Historical Sketches of the Indian Tribes; A Description of American Antiquities . . .* (New York: Mark H. Newman & Co., 1847), page 620.

Page 37 *Illustrated London News*, April 13, 1844.

Page 40 *Harper's Weekly*, July 17, 1875, pp. 590-91.

Page 42 Dallas Historical Society.

Page 43 Geraldine Hagy, Plano.

Page 46 The Institute of Texan Cultures.

Page 48 The Institute of Texan Cultures.

Page 53 Barker Texas History Center, The University of Texas at Austin.

Page 57 Barker Texas History Center, The University of Texas at Austin.

Page 58 Newberry Library, Chicago, Illinois.

Page 62 Amelia Barr, *All the Days of My Life* (New York: D. Appleton & Company, 1913).

Page 64 *Harper's Weekly*, January 22, 1870, p. 61.

Page 65 Alex E. Sweet and J. Armoy Knox, *On a Mexican Mustang Through Texas* (London: Chatto & Windus, 1905).

Page 67 *A History of Texas, Emigrants Guide to The Republic* (New York: Nafes & Cornish, 1844).

Page 69 Houston Public Library.

Page 72 *Harper's New Monthly Magazine* (New York: Harper and Brothers, 1879), vol. 59.

Page 73 Barker Texas History Center, The University of Texas at Austin.

Page 75 *The Texian Advocate*, Victoria, January 11, 1850; *The Indianola Bulletin*.
Page 77 *The Weekly Telegraph*, Houston, April 1, 1857.
Page 78 Both from *The Weekly Telegraph*, Houston, December 28, 1859.
Page 81 *Illustrated London News*, January 4, 1845.
Page 84 Robert H. Williams, *With the Border Ruffians: Memories of the Far West 1852-1868*, ed. E.W. Williams (London: John Murray, 1907).
Page 85 Edouard Charton, ed., *Le Tour du Monde* (Paris: Hachette et Cie, 1863), vol. 2.
Page 87 Library of Congress, Washington, D.C.
Page 88 Dudley Goodall, *A Comprehensive History of Texas* (Dallas: W.G. Scarff, 1898).
Page 89 Amelia E. Barr, *All the Days of My Life* (New York: D. Appleton & Company, 1913).
Page 91 Austin-Travis County Collection, Austin Public Library.
Page 93 Archives Division, Texas State Library, Austin.
Page 95 *Harper's Weekly*, September 27, 1879.
Page 97 Special Collections, University of California at Los Angeles Library.
Page 99 U.S. Dept. of Agriculture Special Report, *Condition of the Sheep Industry*, 1892.
Page 100 Erwin Smith Collection, Library of Congress, Washington, D.C.
Page 101 U.S. Dept. of Agriculture Special Report, *Condition of the Sheep Industry*, 1892.
Page 105 U.S. Dept. of Agriculture Special Report, *Condition of the Sheep Industry*, 1892.
Page 107 Erwin Smith Collection, Library of Congress, Washington, D.C.
Page 109 Unknown
Page 111 Erwin Smith Collection, Library of Congress, Washington, D.C.
Page 112 The Institute of Texan Cultures.
Page 113 *San Angelo Standard Times*, San Angelo.
Page 114 Edith Anson Boulware, San Angelo.
Page 115 Edith Anson Boulware, San Angelo—Edith Anson Boulware, San Angelo.
Page 119 Diamond M Foundation Museum, Snyder.
Page 120 Panhandle-Plains Historical Museum, Canyon.
Page 124 Erwin Smith Collection, Library of Congress, Washington, D.C.
Page 128 H. Leslie Evans, San Antonio.
Page 129 Mrs. James H. Cator, Gruver.
Page 130 Panhandle-Plains Historical Museum, Canyon.
Page 131 Panhandle-Plains Historical Museum, Canyon.
Page 133 Austin-Travis County Collection, Austin Public Library.
Page 134 San Antonio Conservation Society.
Page 135 Mrs. Charles E. Coombes Jr., San Angelo.
Page 136 History of Medicine Collection, The University of Texas Medical Branch Library, Galveston.
Page 139 Morgan Jones Jr., Abilene.
Page 140 Morgan Jones Jr., Abilene—Morgan Jones Jr., Abilene.
Page 141 Marcella Giles Booth, San Antonio.
Page 142 Evelyn Streng Collection, The Institute of Texan Cultures.
Page 143 Palmer Giles, Comfort.
Page 144 Lillie Langtry, *The Days I Knew* (New York: George H. Doran, 1925).
Page 145 H. Leslie Evans, San Antonio.
Page 146 Barker Texas History Center, The University of Texas at Austin.

Page 147 The Dallas *Morning News*; The Dallas *Morning News*.
Page 149 The Institute of Texan Cultures.
Page 150 *San Angelo Standard Times.*
Page 151 Official U.S. Air Force photo—Headquarters San Antonio Air Logistics
          Center, Kelly Air Force Base.
Page 153 Susan Harwell, San Antonio.
Page 154 *The Illustrated London News*, January 18, 1873.

Index

Italic numerals identify photographs.